Machine Learning For Business: A Developer's Cookbook

Written By Richard Aragon

Table of Contents

Chapter 1: Data Preparation

Recipe: Removing Duplicate Rows from a Pandas DataFrame

Use cases:

- This recipe can be used to remove duplicate rows from a Pandas DataFrame. Duplicate rows can occur in a DataFrame for a variety of reasons, such as when data is collected from multiple sources or when data is entered manually. Removing duplicate rows is important to ensure that the data is accurate and consistent.

Function:

The drop_duplicates() method in Pandas can be used to remove duplicate rows from a DataFrame. This method takes the following arguments:

- inplace (boolean): Whether to modify the DataFrame in place (default=False).
- subset (list of strings): A list of column names to check for duplicates.

Best ways to implement:

To remove duplicate rows from a Pandas DataFrame, call the drop_duplicates() method on the DataFrame. Set the inplace parameter to True to modify the DataFrame in place. Optionally, specify the subset of columns to check for duplicates.

Example:

```
import pandas as pd

# Create a Pandas DataFrame
df = pd.DataFrame({'A': [1, 2, 3, 1, 4, 5],
                   'B': [6, 7, 8, 9, 10, 11]})

# Print the DataFrame
print(df)

# Drop duplicate rows
df = df.drop_duplicates(inplace=True)

# Print the DataFrame
print(df)
```

Tips:

- You can also use the unique() method in Pandas to identify the unique values in a DataFrame. This can be useful for debugging purposes or for creating a list of unique values to use in another function.
- If you are working with a large DataFrame, you may want to consider using a distributed computing framework such as Apache Spark to remove duplicate rows. This can significantly improve the performance of the operation.

Recipe: Handling Missing Values in a Pandas DataFrame

Use cases:

This recipe can be used to handle missing values in a Pandas DataFrame. Missing values can occur in a DataFrame for a variety of reasons, such as when data is collected from surveys or when data is entered manually. Handling missing values is important to ensure that the data is accurate and complete.

Function:

There are a variety of ways to handle missing values in a Pandas DataFrame. Some common methods include:

- Dropping rows or columns with missing values
- Filling in missing values with a constant value, such as the mean or median of the column
- Filling in missing values with an interpolated value, such as the value between the previous and next non-missing values

Best ways to implement:

The best way to handle missing values in a Pandas DataFrame will depend on the specific dataset and the intended use of the data. For example, if you are building a machine learning model, you may need to drop rows with missing values or fill in missing values with interpolated values.

Example:

```
import pandas as pd

# Create a Pandas DataFrame with missing values
df = pd.DataFrame({'A': [1, 2, 3, np.nan, 4, 5],
                   'B': [6, 7, 8, 9, np.nan, 11]})

# Print the DataFrame
print(df)

# Drop rows with missing values
df = df.dropna()

# Print the DataFrame
print(df)
```

```
# Fill in missing values with the mean of the column
df['A'].fillna(df['A'].mean(), inplace=True)
df['B'].fillna(df['B'].mean(), inplace=True)

# Print the DataFrame
print(df)
```

Tips:

You can use the isna() and notna() functions in Pandas to identify missing values in a DataFrame.

You can use the fillna() method in Pandas to fill in missing values in a DataFrame. This method takes the following arguments:

- value (object): The value to fill in missing values.
- method (string): The method to use to fill in missing values. Valid methods include ffill (fill forward), bfill (fill backward), and mean (fill with the mean of the column).
- axis (integer): The axis to fill missing values on. Valid values are 0 (fill rows) and 1 (fill columns).

If you are filling in missing values with a constant value, be sure to choose a value that is appropriate for the column. For example, if you are filling in missing values in a column of age values, you may want to fill in the missing values with the mean age of the population.

If you are filling in missing values with an interpolated value, be sure to choose a method that is appropriate for the data. For example, if you are filling in missing values in a column of temperature values, you may want to use a linear interpolation method.

Recipe: Normalizing Data in a Pandas DataFrame

Use cases:

This recipe can be used to normalize data in a Pandas DataFrame. Normalization is the process of scaling data to a specific range, such as 0 to 1 or -1 to 1. Normalizing data is important for some machine learning algorithms, such as support vector machines and neural networks. Function:

There are a variety of ways to normalize data in a Pandas DataFrame. Some common methods include:

- Min-max normalization: This method scales the data to a range of 0 to 1.
- Standard normalization: This method scales the data to have a mean of 0 and a standard deviation of 1.

Best ways to implement:

The best way to normalize data in a Pandas DataFrame will depend on the specific dataset and the intended use of the data. For example, if you are building a machine learning model, you may want to use min-max normalization or standard normalization.

Example:

```
import pandas as pd
from sklearn.preprocessing import MinMaxScaler, StandardScaler

# Create a Pandas DataFrame
df = pd.DataFrame({'A': [1, 2, 3, 4, 5],
                   'B': [6, 7, 8, 9, 10]})

# Print the DataFrame
print(df)

# Normalize the data using min-max normalization
scaler = MinMaxScaler()
df_norm = scaler.fit_transform(df)

# Print the normalized DataFrame
print(df_norm)

# Normalize the data using standard normalization
scaler = StandardScaler()
```

```
df_norm = scaler.fit_transform(df)

# Print the normalized DataFrame
print(df_norm)
```

Tips:

- You can use the fit_transform() method in scikit-learn to normalize data in a Pandas DataFrame. This method takes the DataFrame as input and returns a normalized DataFrame as output.
- You can use the inverse_transform() method in scikit-learn to inverse normalize data in a Pandas DataFrame. This method takes a normalized DataFrame as input and returns the original DataFrame as output.
- When normalizing data, it is important to normalize all of the features in the DataFrame. This will ensure that all of the features are on the same scale and that no one feature has an undue influence on the model.
- If you are using a machine learning algorithm that is sensitive to outliers, you may want to consider removing outliers from the data before normalizing it.

Recipe: Encoding Categorical Data in a Pandas DataFrame

Use cases:

This recipe can be used to encode categorical data in a Pandas DataFrame. Categorical data is data that can be classified into different categories, such as gender, country, or product category. Machine learning algorithms typically cannot work with categorical data directly, so it is necessary to encode the data before training a model.
Function:

There are a variety of ways to encode categorical data in a Pandas DataFrame. Some common methods include:

Label encoding: This method assigns a unique integer to each category.
One-hot encoding: This method creates a new binary feature for each category.

Best ways to implement:

The best way to encode categorical data in a Pandas DataFrame will depend on the specific dataset and the intended use of the data. For example, if you are building a machine learning model, you may want to use label encoding or one-hot encoding.

Example:

```
import pandas as pd

# Create a Pandas DataFrame with categorical data
df = pd.DataFrame({'Country': ['USA', 'UK', 'Germany', 'France', 'China']})

# Print the DataFrame
print(df)

# Encode the categorical data using label encoding
from sklearn.preprocessing import LabelEncoder

le = LabelEncoder()
df['Country_encoded'] = le.fit_transform(df['Country'])

# Print the encoded DataFrame
print(df)

# Encode the categorical data using one-hot encoding
from sklearn.preprocessing import OneHotEncoder
```

```
ohe = OneHotEncoder()
df_onehot = ohe.fit_transform(df[['Country']])

# Print the one-hot encoded DataFrame
print(df_onehot)
```

Tips:

- You can use the fit_transform() method in scikit-learn to encode categorical data in a Pandas DataFrame. This method takes the DataFrame as input and returns an encoded DataFrame as output.
- You can use the inverse_transform() method in scikit-learn to inverse encode categorical data in a Pandas DataFrame. This method takes an encoded DataFrame as input and returns the original DataFrame as output.
- When encoding categorical data, it is important to encode all of the categorical features in the DataFrame. This will ensure that all of the features are on the same scale and that no one feature has an undue influence on the model.
- If you are using a machine learning algorithm that is sensitive to outliers, you may want to consider removing outliers from the data before encoding it.

Recipe: Removing Outliers from a Pandas DataFrame

Use cases:

This recipe can be used to remove outliers from a Pandas DataFrame. Outliers are data points that are significantly different from the rest of the data. Outliers can occur for a variety of reasons, such as human error, data corruption, or natural variation. Removing outliers is important to ensure that the data is accurate and representative of the underlying population. Function:

There are a variety of ways to remove outliers from a Pandas DataFrame. Some common methods include:

- Interquartile range (IQR) method: This method identifies outliers as data points that fall outside of the 1st and 3rd quartiles, plus or minus 1.5 times the IQR.
- Z-score method: This method identifies outliers as data points that have a z-score greater than 3 or less than -3.
- Isolation forest: This is a machine learning algorithm that can be used to detect outliers in data.

Best ways to implement:

The best way to remove outliers from a Pandas DataFrame will depend on the specific dataset and the intended use of the data. For example, if you are building a machine learning model, you may want to use the IQR method or the z-score method.

Example:

```
import pandas as pd

# Create a Pandas DataFrame with outliers
df = pd.DataFrame({'A': [1, 2, 3, 4, 5, 100]})

# Print the DataFrame
print(df)

# Remove outliers using the IQR method
def remove_outliers_IQR(df, col):
  """Removes outliers from a Pandas DataFrame using the IQR method.

  Args:
    df: A Pandas DataFrame.
    col: The column to remove outliers from.
```

```
    Returns:
      A Pandas DataFrame with outliers removed.
    """

    q1 = df[col].quantile(0.25)
    q3 = df[col].quantile(0.75)
    IQR = q3 - q1
    lower_bound = q1 - 1.5 * IQR
    upper_bound = q3 + 1.5 * IQR
    df_filtered = df[df[col] > lower_bound]
    df_filtered = df_filtered[df_filtered[col] < upper_bound]
    return df_filtered

df = remove_outliers_IQR(df, 'A')

# Print the DataFrame with outliers removed
print(df)
```

Recipe: Converting Data to Vector Format in Python

Use cases:

This recipe can be used to convert any Python data type to vector format, including strings, numbers, lists, and dictionaries. This can be useful for machine learning applications, where data is often represented as vectors.

Function:

There are a variety of ways to convert data to vector format in Python. One common method is to use the numpy.array() function. This function takes a Python data structure as input and returns a NumPy array as output.

Best ways to implement:

To convert a Python data structure to vector format using NumPy, simply call the numpy.array() function with the data structure as input. For example, to convert a Python list of numbers to a NumPy array, you would use the following code:

```
import numpy as np

my_list = [1, 2, 3, 4, 5]

# Convert the list to a NumPy array
numpy_array = np.array(my_list)

# Print the NumPy array
print(numpy_array)
```

You can also use the numpy.array() function to convert a Python dictionary to vector format. For example, the following code converts a Python dictionary with a name and age attribute to a NumPy array:

```
import numpy as np

my_dict = {'name': 'John Doe', 'age': 30}

# Convert the dictionary to a NumPy array
numpy_array = np.array([my_dict['name'], my_dict['age']])

# Print the NumPy array
print(numpy_array)
```

If you are working with text data, you may want to use a natural language processing (NLP) library to convert the text to vector format. For example, the following code uses the TensorFlow Hub library to convert a sentence to a vector representation:

```
import tensorflow as tf
import tensorflow_hub as hub

# Load the TensorFlow Hub model
model = hub.load("https://tfhub.dev/google/universal-sentence-encoder-lite/5")

# Convert the sentence to a vector representation
sentence = "This is a sentence."
sentence_vector = model([sentence])

# Print the sentence vector
print(sentence_vector)
```

Tips:

When converting data to vector format, it is important to keep the following in mind:

- Vectors must be of a consistent length. This means that all of the vectors in a dataset must have the same number of elements.
- Vectors can represent different types of data, such as numerical data, text data, and image data.

Recipe: Converting Data to JSON in Python

Use cases:

This recipe can be used to convert any Python data type to JSON, including strings, numbers, lists, dictionaries, and objects. This can be useful for storing data in a compact and readable format, or for sending and receiving data over the web.
Function:

The json module in Python provides a simple way to convert data to JSON. The json.dumps() function takes a Python data structure as input and returns a JSON string as output.
Best ways to implement:

To convert a Python data structure to JSON, simply call the json.dumps() function with the data structure as input. For example, to convert a Python dictionary to JSON, you would use the following code:

```
import json

my_dict = {'name': 'John Doe', 'age': 30}

# Convert the dictionary to JSON
json_string = json.dumps(my_dict)

# Print the JSON string
print(json_string)
```

You can also use the json.dumps() function to convert a Python list to JSON. For example, the following code converts a Python list of strings to JSON:

```
import json

my_list = ['item1', 'item2', 'item3']

# Convert the list to JSON
json_string = json.dumps(my_list)

# Print the JSON string
print(json_string)
```

You can also use the json.dumps() function to convert a Python object to JSON. For example, the following code converts a Python object with a name and age attribute to JSON:

```python
import json

class Person:
  def __init__(self, name, age):
    self.name = name
    self.age = age

my_person = Person('John Doe', 30)

# Convert the object to JSON
json_string = json.dumps(my_person)

# Print the JSON string
print(json_string)
```

Tips:

When converting data to JSON, it is important to keep the following in mind:

- JSON does not support certain Python data types, such as sets and complex numbers. If you attempt to convert a Python data type that is not supported by JSON, you will get an error.
- JSON strings must be enclosed in double quotes.
- JSON key-value pairs must be separated by commas.

Recipe: Feature Engineering

Use cases:

Feature engineering is the process of manipulating and transforming data to create new features that are more informative and predictive for a given machine learning task. Feature engineering can be used to improve the performance of machine learning models by:

- Reducing the dimensionality of the data
- Removing noise from the data
- Creating new features that are more informative and predictive for the target variable

Function:

There are a variety of feature engineering techniques that can be used, depending on the specific dataset and machine learning task. Some common feature engineering techniques include:

- Feature selection: This involves selecting the most informative and predictive features from the dataset.
- Feature transformation: This involves manipulating and transforming the data to create new features. For example; you could create a new feature that represents the ratio of two other features, or you could create a new feature that represents the change in a value over time.
- Feature creation: This involves creating new features from scratch. For example, you could create a new feature that represents the presence or absence of a certain word in a text document.

Best ways to implement:

The best way to implement feature engineering will depend on the specific dataset and machine learning task. However, there are some general best practices that you can follow:

Start by understanding the dataset and the machine learning task. This will help you to identify the most informative and predictive features.
Experiment with different feature engineering techniques and evaluate the performance of your machine learning model on each iteration.
Document the feature engineering techniques that you use so that you can reproduce your results and share your work with others.
Example:

Let's say that we are building a machine learning model to predict whether or not a customer will churn (cancel their subscription). We have a dataset of customer data that includes features such as the customer's age, gender, location, and subscription history.

We could use feature engineering to improve the performance of our machine learning model by creating new features such as:

Customer lifetime value (CLV): This feature represents the total revenue that we expect to generate from a customer over the course of their subscription.
Churn risk score: This feature represents the probability that a customer will churn. We could use a machine learning algorithm to train a churn risk prediction model and then use the predicted churn risk scores as a new feature in our churn prediction model.
Subscription usage patterns: This feature could represent the number of times a customer has logged in to their account in the past month, the number of products they have purchased in the past month, or the amount of money they have spent in the past month.
By creating these new features, we can provide our machine learning model with more informative and predictive data, which can lead to improved performance.

Tips:

When performing feature engineering, it is important to keep the following in mind:

Avoid overfitting: Overfitting is when a machine learning model learns the training data too well and is unable to generalize to new data. To avoid overfitting, it is important to use a validation set to evaluate the performance of your machine learning model on unseen data.
Use domain knowledge: Domain knowledge is your understanding of the specific dataset and machine learning task. Use this knowledge to guide your feature engineering decisions.
Document your work: It is important to document the feature engineering techniques that you use so that you can reproduce your results and share your work with others.

Recipe: Splitting Training and Test Data

Use cases:

Splitting training and test data is an important step in the machine learning process. It helps to ensure that the model is not overfitting the training data and that it is able to generalize to new data.

Function:

To split training and test data, we can use the train_test_split() function in scikit-learn. This function takes the dataset as input and returns two datasets: a training dataset and a test dataset.

Best ways to implement:

The best way to split training and test data will depend on the specific dataset and machine learning task. However, there are some general best practices that you can follow:

- Use a random split: This is the most common way to split training and test data. To perform a random split, we can use the shuffle=True parameter in the train_test_split() function.
- Stratified split: This type of split ensures that the training and test datasets have the same distribution of the target variable. This can be useful for classification tasks. To perform a stratified split, we can use the stratify=y parameter in the train_test_split() function, where y is the target variable.
- Holdout split: This type of split involves setting aside a portion of the data for the test set and using the remaining data for the training set. Holdout splits are typically used for small datasets.

Example:

```
from sklearn.model_selection import train_test_split

# Load the dataset
X = ...
y = ...

# Split the data into training and test sets
X_train, X_test, y_train, y_test = train_test_split(X, y, test_size=0.25)
```

Tips:

When splitting training and test data, it is important to keep the following in mind:

Use a consistent split: It is important to use the same split for all of your experiments. This will help you to compare the performance of different machine learning models fairly.
Use a large enough test set: The test set should be large enough to be representative of the real world data that the model will be used on.
Use a validation set: A validation set can be used to evaluate the performance of the model on unseen data without overfitting the training data.

Chapter 2: Machine Learning Algorithm Recipes

Recipe: Linear Regression

Use cases:

Linear regression is a supervised machine learning algorithm that can be used to predict a continuous target variable. It is a simple but powerful algorithm that can be used for a variety of tasks, such as predicting house prices, predicting customer churn, and predicting stock prices.

Function:

Linear regression models the relationship between a continuous target variable and one or more independent variables. The model is trained by fitting a line to the data points. The line is then used to predict the target variable for new data points.

Best ways to implement:

The best way to implement linear regression will depend on the specific programming language that you are using. However, there are some general best practices that you can follow:

- Use a regularization technique: Regularization techniques help to prevent overfitting. Common regularization techniques for linear regression include L1 regularization and L2 regularization.
- Use a cross-validation technique: Cross-validation techniques help to evaluate the performance of the model on unseen data. Common cross-validation techniques for linear regression include k-fold cross-validation and leave-one-out cross-validation.

Example:
```
import numpy as np
from sklearn.linear_model import LinearRegression

# Load the dataset
X = ...
y = ...

# Create a linear regression model
model = LinearRegression()

# Fit the model to the training data
model.fit(X_train, y_train)
```

```
# Make predictions on the test data
y_pred = model.predict(X_test)

# Evaluate the performance of the model
print(np.mean(np.square(y_test - y_pred)))
```

Tips:

When using linear regression, it is important to keep the following in mind:

- Linear regression models assume that the relationship between the target variable and the independent variables is linear. If the relationship is not linear, then linear regression may not be a good choice of algorithm.
- Linear regression models are sensitive to outliers. It is important to identify and remove outliers from the data before training the model.
- Linear regression models can be overfitted to the training data. It is important to use regularization techniques and cross-validation techniques to prevent overfitting.

Recipe: Logistic Regression

Use cases:

Logistic regression is a supervised machine learning algorithm that can be used to predict a binary target variable. It is a simple but powerful algorithm that can be used for a variety of tasks, such as predicting whether or not a customer will churn, predicting whether or not a patient has a disease, and predicting whether or not an email is spam.

Function:

Logistic regression models the relationship between a binary target variable and one or more independent variables. The model is trained by fitting a logistic function to the data points. The logistic function is then used to predict the probability of the target variable being 1 for new data points.

Best ways to implement:

The best way to implement logistic regression will depend on the specific programming language that you are using. However, there are some general best practices that you can follow:

- Use a regularization technique: Regularization techniques help to prevent overfitting. Common regularization techniques for logistic regression include L1 regularization and L2 regularization.
- Use a cross-validation technique: Cross-validation techniques help to evaluate the performance of the model on unseen data. Common cross-validation techniques for logistic regression include k-fold cross-validation and leave-one-out cross-validation.

Example:

```
import numpy as np
from sklearn.linear_model import LogisticRegression

# Load the dataset
X = ...
y = ...

# Create a logistic regression model
model = LogisticRegression()

# Fit the model to the training data
model.fit(X_train, y_train)
```

```
# Make predictions on the test data
y_pred = model.predict_proba(X_test)[:, 1]

# Evaluate the performance of the model
print(np.mean(y_test == y_pred > 0.5))
```

Tips:

When using logistic regression, it is important to keep the following in mind:

- Logistic regression models assume that the relationship between the target variable and the independent variables is linear in the logit space. If the relationship is not linear, then logistic regression may not be a good choice of algorithm.
- Logistic regression models are sensitive to outliers. It is important to identify and remove outliers from the data before training the model.
- Logistic regression models can be overfitted to the training data. It is important to use regularization techniques and cross-validation techniques to prevent overfitting.

Recipe: Decision Trees

Use cases:

Decision trees are supervised machine learning algorithms that can be used for both classification and regression tasks. They are easy to interpret and can be used to model complex relationships between the target variable and the independent variables.

Function:

Decision trees work by recursively partitioning the data into smaller and smaller subsets until each subset contains only data points with the same target value. The algorithm then constructs a tree model that represents the decision-making process used to partition the data.
Best ways to implement:

The best way to implement decision trees will depend on the specific programming language that you are using. However, there are some general best practices that you can follow:

- Use a pruning technique: Pruning techniques help to prevent overfitting. Common pruning techniques for decision trees include pre-pruning and post-pruning.
- Use a cross-validation technique: Cross-validation techniques help to evaluate the performance of the model on unseen data. Common cross-validation techniques for decision trees include k-fold cross-validation and leave-one-out cross-validation.

Example:
```
from sklearn.tree import DecisionTreeClassifier

# Load the dataset
X = ...
y = ...

# Create a decision tree classifier model
model = DecisionTreeClassifier()

# Fit the model to the training data
model.fit(X_train, y_train)

# Make predictions on the test data
y_pred = model.predict(X_test)

# Evaluate the performance of the model
print(np.mean(y_pred == y_test))
```

Tips:

When using decision trees, it is important to keep the following in mind:

- Decision trees can be overfitted to the training data. It is important to use pruning techniques and cross-validation techniques to prevent overfitting.
- Decision trees can be sensitive to outliers. It is important to identify and remove outliers from the data before training the model.
- Decision trees can be difficult to interpret for large datasets.

Recipe: Naive Bayes

Use cases:

Naive Bayes is a supervised machine learning algorithm that can be used for both classification and regression tasks. Naive Bayes is a simple but powerful algorithm that is well-suited for tasks where the independent variables are relatively independent of each other.
Function:

Naive Bayes works by using Bayes' theorem to calculate the probability of the target variable given the independent variables. Bayes' theorem is a mathematical formula that allows us to calculate the probability of one event happening given that another event has already happened.

Best ways to implement:

The best way to implement Naive Bayes will depend on the specific programming language that you are using. However, there are some general best practices that you can follow:

- Use a smoothing technique: Smoothing techniques help to prevent overfitting by preventing the model from assigning too much weight to data points that are rare in the training data. Common smoothing techniques for Naive Bayes include Laplace smoothing and Lidstone smoothing.
- Use a cross-validation technique: Cross-validation techniques help to evaluate the performance of the model on unseen data. Common cross-validation techniques for Naive Bayes include k-fold cross-validation and leave-one-out cross-validation.

Example:

```
import numpy as np
from sklearn.naive_bayes import GaussianNB

# Load the dataset
X = ...
y = ...

# Create a Naive Bayes classifier
model = GaussianNB()

# Fit the model to the training data
model.fit(X_train, y_train)

# Make predictions on the test data
```

```
y_pred = model.predict(X_test)

# Evaluate the performance of the model
print(np.mean(y_test == y_pred))
```

Tips:

When using Naive Bayes, it is important to keep the following in mind:

- Naive Bayes assumes that the independent variables are independent of each other. If the independent variables are not independent, then Naive Bayes may not be a good choice of algorithm.
- Naive Bayes can be sensitive to outliers. It is important to identify and remove outliers from the data before training the model.
- Naive Bayes can be overfitted to the training data. It is important to use smoothing techniques and cross-validation techniques to prevent overfitting.

Recipe: Random Forests

Use cases:

Random forests are a supervised machine learning algorithm that can be used for both classification and regression tasks. Random forests are an ensemble learning algorithm, which means that they combine the predictions of multiple individual machine learning models to produce a final prediction.

Function:

Random forests work by constructing a collection of decision trees. Each decision tree is trained on a different subset of the data, and each decision tree uses a different random sample of the features. The predictions of the individual decision trees are then averaged to produce the final prediction of the random forest model.

Best ways to implement:

The best way to implement random forests will depend on the specific programming language that you are using. However, there are some general best practices that you can follow:

- Use a large number of trees: The more trees in the random forest, the more accurate the model will be. However, using a large number of trees can also make the model slower to train and predict.
- Use a variety of hyperparameters: Random forests have a number of hyperparameters that can be tuned to improve the performance of the model. Common hyperparameters for random forests include the number of trees, the maximum tree depth, and the minimum number of samples required to split a node.
- Use a cross-validation technique: Cross-validation techniques help to evaluate the performance of the model on unseen data. Common cross-validation techniques for random forests include k-fold cross-validation and leave-one-out cross-validation.

Example:
from sklearn.ensemble import RandomForestClassifier

```
# Load the dataset
X = ...
y = ...

# Create a random forest classifier
model = RandomForestClassifier(n_estimators=100)

# Fit the model to the training data
```

```
model.fit(X_train, y_train)

# Make predictions on the test data
y_pred = model.predict(X_test)

# Evaluate the performance of the model
print(np.mean(y_test == y_pred))
```

Tips:

When using random forests, it is important to keep the following in mind:

- Random forests are very robust to overfitting. However, it is still a good idea to use cross-validation techniques to evaluate the performance of the model on unseen data.
- Random forests can be computationally expensive to train. However, there are a number of techniques that can be used to speed up the training process, such as using subsampling and parallelization.

Recipe: K-means Clustering

Use cases:

K-means clustering is an unsupervised machine learning algorithm that can be used to group similar data points together. K-means clustering is a simple and efficient algorithm that is well-suited for a variety of tasks, such as customer segmentation, product recommendation, and image segmentation.

Function:

K-means clustering works by partitioning the data into a predefined number of clusters (K). The algorithm then assigns each data point to the closest cluster. The algorithm iterates until no data points change clusters.

Best ways to implement:

The best way to implement K-means clustering will depend on the specific programming language that you are using. However, there are some general best practices that you can follow:

- Choose the right value for K: The number of clusters (K) is a hyperparameter that needs to be tuned. There are a number of methods that can be used to tune the value of K, such as the elbow method and the silhouette score.
- Normalize the data: Normalizing the data can help to improve the performance of the K-means clustering algorithm. Normalization can be done by scaling each feature to have a mean of 0 and a standard deviation of 1.
- Initialize the centroids carefully: The initial centroids can have a significant impact on the performance of the K-means clustering algorithm. There are a number of ways to initialize the centroids, such as randomly selecting data points or using a more sophisticated method such as K-means++ initialization.

Example:

```
import numpy as np
from sklearn.cluster import KMeans

# Load the dataset
X = ...

# Create a KMeans clusterer with 3 clusters
kmeans = KMeans(n_clusters=3)

# Fit the clusterer to the data
```

```
kmeans.fit(X)

# Predict the cluster labels for each data point
cluster_labels = kmeans.predict(X)

# Print the cluster labels
print(cluster_labels)
```

Tips:

When using K-means clustering, it is important to keep the following in mind:

- K-means clustering is a sensitive algorithm to outliers. It is important to identify and remove outliers from the data before running the algorithm.
- K-means clustering can be overfitted to the training data. It is important to use techniques such as k-fold cross-validation to evaluate the performance of the algorithm on unseen data.

Recipe: Hierarchical Clustering

Use cases:

Hierarchical clustering is an unsupervised machine learning algorithm that can be used to group similar data points together. Hierarchical clustering is a flexible algorithm that can be used to create a variety of different cluster structures, such as dendrograms and tree diagrams.

Function:

Hierarchical clustering works by building a hierarchy of clusters. The algorithm starts by placing each data point in its own cluster. The algorithm then iteratively merges the two closest clusters until a single cluster remains.

Best ways to implement:

The best way to implement hierarchical clustering will depend on the specific programming language that you are using. However, there are some general best practices that you can follow:

- Choose the right distance metric: The distance metric is used to calculate the distance between two data points. The choice of distance metric can have a significant impact on the cluster structure that is produced by the algorithm. Some common distance metrics for hierarchical clustering include the Euclidean distance and the Manhattan distance.
- Choose the right linkage criterion: The linkage criterion is used to determine which two clusters to merge at each step of the algorithm. Some common linkage criteria for hierarchical clustering include single linkage, complete linkage, and average linkage.
- Cut the dendrogram at the right height: The dendrogram is a tree diagram that represents the hierarchy of clusters. The height at which the dendrogram is cut determines the number of clusters in the final solution. There are a number of methods that can be used to cut the dendrogram, such as the elbow method and the silhouette score.

Example:
```
import numpy as np
from scipy.cluster.hierarchy import linkage

# Load the dataset
X = ...

# Compute the distance matrix
distance_matrix = linkage(X, method='euclidean')
```

```
# Cut the dendrogram at a height of 2
cut_dendrogram = linkage(distance_matrix, method='ward', criterion='distance')

# Get the cluster labels
cluster_labels = cut_dendrogram[:, 0]

# Print the cluster labels
print(cluster_labels)
```

Tips:

When using hierarchical clustering, it is important to keep the following in mind:

- Hierarchical clustering can be computationally expensive for large datasets.
- Hierarchical clustering can be sensitive to outliers. It is important to identify and remove outliers from the data before running the algorithm.
- Hierarchical clustering can be overfitted to the training data. It is important to use techniques such as k-fold cross-validation to evaluate the performance of the algorithm on unseen data.

Recipe: Gaussian Mixture Models

Use cases:

Gaussian mixture models (GMMs) are a type of unsupervised machine learning algorithm that can be used to model the probability distribution of a dataset. GMMs are a flexible algorithm that can be used to model a variety of different probability distributions, including multimodal distributions and distributions with complex shapes.

Function:

GMMs work by modeling the dataset as a mixture of Gaussian distributions. Each Gaussian distribution represents a different cluster in the data. The algorithm estimates the parameters of the Gaussian distributions, such as the mean and covariance, using the expectation-maximization (EM) algorithm.

Best ways to implement:

The best way to implement GMMs will depend on the specific programming language that you are using. However, there are some general best practices that you can follow:

- Choose the right number of components: The number of components in the GMM is a hyperparameter that needs to be tuned. There are a number of methods that can be used to tune the number of components, such as the Bayesian information criterion (BIC) and the Akaike information criterion (AIC).
- Initialize the model parameters carefully: The initial model parameters can have a significant impact on the performance of the GMM. There are a number of ways to initialize the model parameters, such as randomly selecting data points or using a more sophisticated method such as k-means++ initialization.

Example:
```
import numpy as np
from sklearn.mixture import GaussianMixture

# Load the dataset
X = ...

# Create a GMM with 3 components
gmm = GaussianMixture(n_components=3)

# Fit the model to the data
gmm.fit(X)
```

```
# Predict the cluster labels for each data point
cluster_labels = gmm.predict(X)

# Print the cluster labels
print(cluster_labels)
```

Tips:

When using GMMs, it is important to keep the following in mind:

- GMMs can be sensitive to outliers. It is important to identify and remove outliers from the data before running the algorithm.
- GMMs can be overfitted to the training data. It is important to use techniques such as k-fold cross-validation to evaluate the performance of the algorithm on unseen data.

Recipe: Apriori Algorithm

Use cases:

The Apriori algorithm is a type of unsupervised machine learning algorithm that can be used to find association rules in data. Association rules are relationships between different items in a dataset that occur together frequently. Apriori is a simple but powerful algorithm that can be used to identify a variety of different association rules, such as product recommendations and customer segmentation.

Function:

The Apriori algorithm works by generating a set of candidate itemsets. An itemset is a set of items that occur together frequently in the dataset. The algorithm then prunes the candidate itemsets to remove any itemsets that are not frequent enough. The algorithm then generates a new set of candidate itemsets and prunes them again. This process continues until no new candidate itemsets can be generated.

Best ways to implement:

The best way to implement the Apriori algorithm will depend on the specific programming language that you are using. However, there are some general best practices that you can follow:

- Choose the right support threshold: The support threshold is a hyperparameter that determines the minimum frequency of an itemset in the dataset for it to be considered frequent. The choice of support threshold can have a significant impact on the number of association rules that are found.
- Use a hash table to store the itemsets: A hash table can be used to store the itemsets efficiently and to quickly check if an itemset is frequent.

Example:

```
import numpy as np
from apyori import apriori

# Load the dataset
transactions = ...

# Create an apriori object
apriori_object = apriori(transactions, min_support=0.2, min_confidence=0.5)

# Generate the association rules
```

```
association_rules = list(apriori_object)

# Print the association rules
for rule in association_rules:
    print(rule)
```

Tips:

When using the Apriori algorithm, it is important to keep the following in mind:

- The Apriori algorithm can be computationally expensive for large datasets.
- The Apriori algorithm can be sensitive to outliers. It is important to identify and remove outliers from the data before running the algorithm.
- The Apriori algorithm can be overfitted to the training data. It is important to use techniques such as k-fold cross-validation to evaluate the performance of the algorithm on unseen data.

Recipe: FP-Growth Algorithm

Use cases:

The FP-growth algorithm is a type of unsupervised machine learning algorithm that can be used to find association rules in data. Association rules are relationships between different items in a dataset that occur together frequently. FP-growth is a faster and more efficient algorithm than the Apriori algorithm, especially for large datasets.

Function:

The FP-growth algorithm works by first constructing an FP-tree from the dataset. The FP-tree is a tree-like structure that represents the frequent itemsets in the dataset. Once the FP-tree is constructed, the algorithm recursively mines the FP-tree to find association rules.

Best ways to implement:

The best way to implement the FP-growth algorithm will depend on the specific programming language that you are using. However, there are some general best practices that you can follow:

- Choose the right minimum support threshold: The minimum support threshold is a hyperparameter that determines the minimum frequency of an itemset in the dataset for it to be considered frequent. The choice of minimum support threshold can have a significant impact on the number of association rules that are found.
- Prune the FP-tree: The FP-tree can be pruned to remove any infrequent itemsets. This can improve the performance of the algorithm, especially for large datasets.

Example:
```
import numpy as np
from mlxtend.frequent_patterns import fp_growth

# Load the dataset
transactions = ...

# Create an fp_growth object
fp_growth_object = fp_growth(transactions, min_support=0.2)

# Find the association rules
association_rules = fp_growth_object.get_rules()

# Print the association rules
for rule in association_rules:
```

```
print(rule)
```

Tips:

When using the FP-growth algorithm, it is important to keep the following in mind:

The FP-growth algorithm is faster and more efficient than the Apriori algorithm, especially for large datasets.
The FP-growth algorithm can be sensitive to outliers. It is important to identify and remove outliers from the data before running the algorithm.
The FP-growth algorithm can be overfitted to the training data. It is important to use techniques such as k-fold cross-validation to evaluate the performance of the algorithm on unseen data.

Recipe: Principal Component Analysis (PCA)

Use cases:

PCA is an unsupervised machine learning algorithm that can be used for dimensionality reduction, data visualization, and anomaly detection. PCA is a simple but powerful algorithm that can be used to improve the performance of other machine learning algorithms by reducing the number of features in the data.
Function:

PCA works by finding a new set of orthogonal features, called principal components, that explain the maximum amount of variance in the data. The principal components are found by computing the eigenvectors of the covariance matrix of the data. The eigenvectors are the directions in which the data varies the most.

Best ways to implement:

The best way to implement PCA will depend on the specific programming language that you are using. However, there are some general best practices that you can follow:

- Standardize the data: It is important to standardize the data before running PCA. This will ensure that all of the features have the same scale and that no one feature dominates the analysis.
- Choose the right number of principal components: The number of principal components to choose is a hyperparameter that needs to be tuned. There are a number of methods that can be used to tune the number of principal components, such as the scree plot and the cumulative variance explained plot.

Example:

```
import numpy as np
from sklearn.decomposition import PCA

# Load the dataset
X = ...

# Create a PCA object
pca = PCA(n_components=2)

# Fit the PCA object to the data
pca.fit(X)

# Transform the data using the PCA object
```

```
X_transformed = pca.transform(X)

# Print the transformed data
print(X_transformed)
```

Tips:

When using PCA, it is important to keep the following in mind:

- PCA is a linear algorithm. If the data is non-linear, then PCA may not be a good choice of algorithm.
- PCA is sensitive to outliers. It is important to identify and remove outliers from the data before running PCA.
- PCA can be overfitted to the training data. It is important to use techniques such as k-fold cross-validation to evaluate the performance of PCA on unseen data.

Recipe: T-Distributed Stochastic Neighbor Embedding (t-SNE)

Use cases:

t-SNE is an unsupervised machine learning algorithm that can be used for dimensionality reduction and data visualization. t-SNE is a non-linear algorithm that can be used to visualize high-dimensional data in a low-dimensional space, such as 2D or 3D.

Function:

t-SNE works by constructing a probability distribution over pairs of high-dimensional objects in such a way that similar objects are assigned a higher probability while dissimilar points are assigned a lower probability. The algorithm then defines a similar probability distribution over the points in the low-dimensional map, and it minimizes the Kullback–Leibler divergence (KL divergence) between the two distributions with respect to the locations of the points in the map.

Best ways to implement:

The best way to implement t-SNE will depend on the specific programming language that you are using. However, there are some general best practices that you can follow:

- Standardize the data: It is important to standardize the data before running t-SNE. This will ensure that all of the features have the same scale and that no one feature dominates the analysis.
- Choose the right perplexity: The perplexity is a hyperparameter that controls the number of neighbors that each point has. The choice of perplexity can have a significant impact on the results of t-SNE.

Example:

```
import numpy as np
from sklearn.manifold import TSNE

# Load the dataset
X = ...

# Create a t-SNE object
tsne = TSNE(n_components=2, perplexity=30)

# Fit the t-SNE object to the data
tsne.fit(X)

# Transform the data using the t-SNE object
```

```
X_transformed = tsne.transform(X)

# Print the transformed data
print(X_transformed)
```

Tips:

When using t-SNE, it is important to keep the following in mind:

- t-SNE is a non-linear algorithm. This means that it can be used to visualize non-linear data.
- t-SNE is sensitive to outliers. It is important to identify and remove outliers from the data before running t-SNE.
- t-SNE can be overfitted to the training data. It is important to use techniques such as k-fold cross-validation to evaluate the performance of t-SNE on unseen data.

Recipe: Uniform Manifold Approximation and Projection (UMAP)

Use cases:

UMAP is an unsupervised machine learning algorithm that can be used for dimensionality reduction and data visualization. UMAP is a non-linear algorithm that can be used to visualize high-dimensional data in a low-dimensional space, such as 2D or 3D. UMAP is particularly well-suited for visualizing data that is distributed on a manifold.

Function:

UMAP works by constructing a fuzzy topological structure of the high-dimensional data. This fuzzy topological structure represents the relationships between the different data points. UMAP then finds a low-dimensional projection of the data that preserves the fuzzy topological structure as much as possible.

Best ways to implement:

The best way to implement UMAP will depend on the specific programming language that you are using. However, there are some general best practices that you can follow:

- Standardize the data: It is important to standardize the data before running UMAP. This will ensure that all of the features have the same scale and that no one feature dominates the analysis.
- Choose the right number of neighbors: The number of neighbors is a hyperparameter that controls how much of the local structure of the data is preserved in the projection. The choice of number of neighbors can have a significant impact on the results of UMAP.
- Choose the right minimum distance: The minimum distance is a hyperparameter that controls how much of the global structure of the data is preserved in the projection. The choice of minimum distance can have a significant impact on the results of UMAP.

Example:

```
import numpy as np
import umap

# Load the dataset
X = ...

# Create a UMAP object
umap = umap.UMAP(n_neighbors=15, min_dist=0.1)

# Fit the UMAP object to the data
```

```
umap.fit(X)

# Transform the data using the UMAP object
X_transformed = umap.transform(X)

# Print the transformed data
print(X_transformed)
```

Tips:

When using UMAP, it is important to keep the following in mind:

- UMAP is a non-linear algorithm. This means that it can be used to visualize non-linear data.
- UMAP is particularly well-suited for visualizing data that is distributed on a manifold.
- UMAP is sensitive to outliers. It is important to identify and remove outliers from the data before running UMAP.
- UMAP can be overfitted to the training data. It is important to use techniques such as k-fold cross-validation to evaluate the performance of UMAP on unseen data.

Chapter 3: LLM Specific Recipes

Recipe: Using Pre Trained LLMs to Fine-Tune for Specific Tasks

Use cases:

This recipe is useful for developers who want to use pre-trained LLMs to fine-tune for specific tasks, such as question answering, code generation, or summarization.
Fine-tuning a pre-trained LLM can be a much faster and more efficient way to develop a high-performing model for a specific task than training an LLM from scratch.

Function:

To fine-tune a pre trained LLM for a specific task, you can use the following steps:
Choose a pre-trained LLM that is appropriate for the task that you want to fine-tune it for. For example, if you want to fine-tune a model for question answering, you might choose a pre-trained LLM that is trained on a dataset of question-answer pairs.
Collect a dataset of training data for the task that you want to fine-tune the model for. This dataset should be labeled with the desired output for each input.
Fine-tune the pretrained LLM on your training dataset. This can be done using a variety of different methods, such as gradient descent or backpropagation.
Evaluate the fine-tuned model on a held-out test dataset to ensure that it is performing well.

Best ways to implement:

The best way to implement this recipe will depend on the specific LLM and fine-tuning method that you are using. However, there are some general best practices that you can follow:

- Use a small learning rate: When fine-tuning a pre-trained LLM, it is important to use a small learning rate. This will help to prevent the model from overfitting to the training data.
- Use a regularization technique: Regularization techniques, such as L1 or L2 regularization, can help to prevent the model from overfitting to the training data.
- Use a large batch size: Using a large batch size can help to improve the performance of the fine-tuning process.
- Use a distributed training library: If you are training a large LLM, you may need to use a distributed training library, such as PyTorch Lightning or Horovod, to train the model on multiple GPUs.

Example:

```
import numpy as np
import torch
from transformers import AutoModelForQuestionAnswering

# Load the pretrained LLM
model = AutoModelForQuestionAnswering.from_pretrained("bert-base-uncased")

# Collect the training data
training_data = ... # A list of question-answer pairs

# Fine-tune the model
model.train()
optimizer = torch.optim.Adam(model.parameters(), lr=1e-5)
for epoch in range(10):
    for batch in training_data:
        loss = model(batch)
        optimizer.zero_grad()
        loss.backward()
        optimizer.step()

# Evaluate the fine-tuned model
model.eval()
test_data = ... # A list of question-answer pairs
accuracy = 0
for batch in test_data:
    outputs = model(batch)
    predictions = outputs.start_logits.argmax(dim=1)
    labels = batch["labels"]
    accuracy += (predictions == labels).sum().item()
accuracy /= len(test_data)
print("Accuracy:", accuracy)
```

Tips:

When fine-tuning a pre trained LLM, it is important to keep the following in mind:

- Fine-tuning a pre-trained LLM can be a computationally expensive process.
- It is important to use a good regularization technique to prevent the model from overfitting to the training data.
- It is important to evaluate the fine-tuned model on a held-out test dataset to ensure that it is performing well.

Recipe: Using RAG Augmentation for LLM Models

Use cases:

RAG augmentation can be used to improve the performance of LLMs on a variety of tasks, such as question answering, summarization, and translation.
RAG augmentation can be particularly useful for tasks where the LLM does not have enough training data, or where the training data is noisy or incomplete.

Function:

RAG augmentation works by providing the LLM with additional information from a knowledge source at inference time. This additional information can be used by the LLM to generate more accurate and informative responses.
To use RAG augmentation, you can use the following steps:
Choose a knowledge source that is relevant to the task that you are using the LLM for. For example, if you are using the LLM for question answering, you might choose a knowledge source that contains a large dataset of question-answer pairs.
Build a retrieval model that can retrieve relevant documents from the knowledge source.
Integrate the retrieval model with the LLM. This can be done using a variety of different methods, such as fine-tuning the LLM on the retrieval results or using a prompt-based approach.

Best ways to implement:

The best way to implement RAG augmentation will depend on the specific LLM and retrieval model that you are using. However, there are some general best practices that you can follow:

- Use a large and diverse knowledge source: The larger and more diverse the knowledge source, the better the LLM will be able to perform.
- Use a powerful retrieval model: The retrieval model should be able to retrieve relevant documents from the knowledge source quickly and efficiently.
- Fine-tune the LLM on the retrieval results: This is the most effective way to integrate the retrieval model with the LLM. However, it can be computationally expensive.
- Use a prompt-based approach: This is a less computationally expensive way to integrate the retrieval model with the LLM. However, it is not as effective as fine-tuning the LLM on the retrieval results.

Example:

```
import numpy as np
import torch
from transformers import AutoModelForQuestionAnswering
```

```
from haystack.document_stores import FAISSDocumentStore
from haystack.pipelines import RagQuestionAnswerer

# Load the pretrained LLM
model = AutoModelForQuestionAnswering.from_pretrained("bert-base-uncased")

# Load the knowledge source
document_store = FAISSDocumentStore()
document_store.update(
    documents=[
        {"content": "This is the first document in the knowledge source."},
        {"content": "This is the second document in the knowledge source."},
    ]
)

# Create a RAG question answering pipeline
pipeline = RagQuestionAnswerer(
    model=model, retriever=document_store
)

# Query the pipeline
question = "What is the capital of France?"
answer = pipeline.predict(question)

# Print the answer
print(answer)
```

This example uses a prompt-based approach to integrate the retrieval model with the LLM. The prompt-based approach works by providing the LLM with a prompt that contains the question and the retrieval results. The LLM then generates an answer based on the prompt.

Tips:

When using RAG augmentation, it is important to keep the following in mind:

- RAG augmentation can improve the performance of LLMs on a variety of tasks, but it is important to choose the right knowledge source and retrieval model for the task that you are using the LLM for.
- Fine-tuning the LLM on the retrieval results is the most effective way to integrate the retrieval model with the LLM, but it can be computationally expensive.
- A prompt-based approach is a less computationally expensive way to integrate the retrieval model with the LLM, but it is not as effective as fine-tuning the LLM on the retrieval results.

Recipe: Quantizing an LLM Model

Use cases:

Quantizing an LLM model can reduce the model's size and memory footprint, making it easier to deploy on resource-constrained devices.
Quantizing an LLM model can also improve the model's inference speed, making it faster to generate predictions.

Function:

Quantization works by reducing the precision of the model's parameters and weights. This can be done without sacrificing too much accuracy by using a variety of different techniques, such as post-training quantization and quantized training.

Best ways to implement:

The best way to implement quantization will depend on the specific LLM that you are using and the framework that you are using to train and deploy the model. However, there are some general best practices that you can follow:

- Choose the right quantization technique: There are a variety of different quantization techniques available, each with its own advantages and disadvantages. It is important to choose the right quantization technique for the specific LLM and task that you are working with.
- Evaluate the model's accuracy after quantization: It is important to evaluate the model's accuracy after quantization to ensure that the loss in accuracy is acceptable.
- Use a calibration step: A calibration step can be used to improve the accuracy of the quantized model.

Example:
```
import numpy as np
import torch
from transformers import AutoModelForQuestionAnswering, QATrainer

# Load the pretrained LLM
model = AutoModelForQuestionAnswering.from_pretrained("bert-base-uncased")

# Quantize the model
trainer = QATrainer(model)
trainer.train()

# Evaluate the quantized model
```

```
model.eval()
test_data = ... # A list of question-answer pairs
accuracy = 0
for batch in test_data:
    outputs = model(batch)
    predictions = outputs.start_logits.argmax(dim=1)
    labels = batch["labels"]
    accuracy += (predictions == labels).sum().item()
accuracy /= len(test_data)
print("Accuracy:", accuracy)
```

This example uses the QATrainer class from the Hugging Face Transformers library to quantize the LLM model. The QATrainer class implements a variety of different quantization techniques, such as post-training quantization and quantized training.

Tips:

When quantizing an LLM model, it is important to keep the following in mind:

- Quantization can reduce the model's size and memory footprint, but it can also lead to a loss in accuracy. It is important to choose the right quantization technique and to evaluate the model's accuracy after quantization to ensure that the loss in accuracy is acceptable.
- Quantization can also improve the model's inference speed. However, the amount of improvement will depend on the specific LLM and task that you are working with.
- Quantization can be a complex process, and it is important to have a good understanding of the different quantization techniques available before getting started.

Recipe: Adding a Variable Attention Mechanism to a Model

Use cases:

Adding a variable attention mechanism to a model can improve the model's performance on a variety of tasks, such as question answering, summarization, and translation.
Variable attention mechanisms can allow the model to focus on different parts of the input depending on the task at hand.

Function:

Variable attention mechanisms work by computing a weight for each token in the input sequence. These weights are then used to create a weighted sum of the input tokens. The weighted sum is then used as the input to the next layer of the model.
The weights for each token are computed using a variety of different methods, such as scaled dot-product attention and additive attention. The specific method that is used will depend on the architecture of the model.

Best ways to implement:

The best way to implement a variable attention mechanism will depend on the specific model that you are using and the framework that you are using to train and deploy the model. However, there are some general best practices that you can follow:

Choose the right attention mechanism: There are a variety of different attention mechanisms available, each with its own advantages and disadvantages. It is important to choose the right attention mechanism for the specific model and task that you are working with.
Implement the attention mechanism efficiently: Attention mechanisms can be computationally expensive, so it is important to implement them efficiently. This can be done by using a variety of techniques, such as caching and parallelization.

Example:
```
import numpy as np
import torch
from transformers import AutoModelForQuestionAnswering, AutoModelWithLMHead

# Load the pretrained LLM
model = AutoModelForQuestionAnswering.from_pretrained("bert-base-uncased")

# Add a variable attention mechanism to the model
class MyModel(AutoModelWithLMHead):
    def __init__(self, config):
        super().__init__(config)
```

```
        # Add a variable attention mechanism
        self.attention = torch.nn.MultiheadAttention(config.hidden_size,
config.num_attention_heads)

    def forward(self, input_ids, attention_mask=None, labels=None):
        outputs = super().forward(input_ids, attention_mask=attention_mask, labels=labels)

        # Apply the variable attention mechanism
        hidden_states = outputs.last_hidden_state
        attention_output, _ = self.attention(hidden_states, hidden_states, hidden_states)

        # Use the attention output as the input to the next layer of the model
        outputs.last_hidden_state = attention_output

        return outputs

# Create a new instance of the model
new_model = MyModel.from_pretrained("bert-base-uncased")

# Fine-tune the model on a question answering dataset
# ...

# Evaluate the fine-tuned model on a held-out test dataset
# ...
```

This example shows how to add a variable attention mechanism to the BERT model. The variable attention mechanism is implemented using the torch.nn.MultiheadAttention class. The MultiheadAttention class implements a variety of different attention mechanisms, such as scaled dot-product attention and additive attention.

Tips:

When adding a variable attention mechanism to a model, it is important to keep the following in mind:

- Variable attention mechanisms can improve the model's performance on a variety of tasks, but they can also add complexity to the model and make it more difficult to train. It is important to choose the right attention mechanism for the specific model and task that you are working with.
- Variable attention mechanisms can be computationally expensive, so it is important to implement them efficiently.

- It is important to evaluate the model's performance on a held-out test dataset after adding a variable attention mechanism to ensure that the improvement in performance is statistically significant.

Recipe: Making a POST API Call to an LLM Model

Use cases:

Making a POST API call to an LLM model can allow you to use the model to generate text, translate languages, or answer questions from your own application.
This can be useful for a variety of tasks, such as developing chatbots, virtual assistants, and other AI-powered applications.

Function:

To make a POST API call to an LLM model, you will need to know the following:

The URL of the API endpoint
The request body
The authorization header
The request body should contain the text that you want the LLM model to process. The authorization header should contain your API key or token.

Best ways to implement:

The best way to implement this recipe will depend on the programming language that you are using. However, there are some general best practices that you can follow:

- Use a library for making HTTP requests: There are a variety of libraries available for making HTTP requests in different programming languages. These libraries can make it easier to make and manage API calls.
- Use a JSON parser to serialize and deserialize the request and response bodies: JSON is a common format for exchanging data over HTTP APIs. Using a JSON parser can make it easier to serialize and deserialize the request and response bodies.
- Handle errors: It is important to handle errors that may occur when making an API call. This can be done by using a try/except block or by using a library for handling HTTP errors.

Example:
```
import requests
import json

# The URL of the API endpoint
API_ENDPOINT = "https://api.example.com/v1/generate"

# The request body
request_body = {
```

```
  "text": "Write a poem about a cat."
}

# The authorization header
authorization_header = {"Authorization": "Bearer YOUR_API_KEY"}

# Make the POST API call
response = requests.post(
    API_ENDPOINT,
    headers=authorization_header,
    json=request_body
)

# Check the status code
if response.status_code == 200:
    # Success!
    response_body = json.loads(response.content)

    # Print the generated text
    print(response_body["text"])
else:
    # Error!
    print(response.status_code, response.reason)
```

This example shows how to make a POST API call to an LLM model to generate text. The example uses the Python requests library to make the HTTP request and the JSON library to serialize and deserialize the request and response bodies.

Tips:

When making a POST API call to an LLM model, it is important to keep the following in mind:

- The specific format of the request and response bodies will vary depending on the API that you are using. It is important to consult the API documentation for more information.
- Some APIs may require you to authenticate before making a request. This can be done by providing an API key or token in the authorization header.
- It is important to handle errors that may occur when making an API call. This can be done by using a try/except block or by using a library for handling HTTP errors.

Recipe: Creating a Hosted Endpoint for an LLM Model

Use cases:

Creating a hosted endpoint for an LLM model allows you to share your model with others and make it easier for them to use.
This can be useful for a variety of tasks, such as developing chatbots, virtual assistants, and other AI-powered applications.

Function:

To create a hosted endpoint for an LLM model, you will need to:
Choose a hosting provider: There are a variety of hosting providers available, such as Google Cloud Platform, Amazon Web Services, and Microsoft Azure.
Deploy your model to the hosting provider: This process will vary depending on the hosting provider that you choose.
Create an API endpoint: This can be done using a variety of tools and technologies, such as Flask, Django, or FastAPI.
Implement the API endpoint: The API endpoint should accept requests and return responses in a format that is compatible with your model.
Best ways to implement:

The best way to implement this recipe will depend on the hosting provider that you choose and the programming language that you are using. However, there are some general best practices that you can follow:

- Use a framework to develop your API endpoint: Frameworks such as Flask, Django, and FastAPI can make it easier to develop and maintain your API endpoint.
- Use a version control system: Version control systems such as Git can help you to track changes to your code and roll back to previous versions if necessary.
- Use documentation tools: Documentation tools can help you to document your API endpoint and make it easier for others to use.

Example:
from flask import Flask, request, jsonify

# Load the LLM model
model = ...

# Create a Flask app
app = Flask(__name__)

Define the API endpoint

```python
@app.route("/generate", methods=["POST"])
def generate():
    # Get the text from the request body
    text = request.get_json()["text"]

    # Generate text using the LLM model
    generated_text = model.generate(text)

    # Return the generated text as a JSON response
    return jsonify({"text": generated_text})

# Start the Flask app
if __name__ == "__main__":
    app.run(host="0.0.0.0", port=8080)
```

This example shows how to create a hosted endpoint for an LLM model using the Flask framework. The API endpoint accepts a JSON request body with the text that you want the LLM model to generate. The API endpoint then generates text using the LLM model and returns the generated text as a JSON response.

Tips:

When creating a hosted endpoint for an LLM model, it is important to keep the following in mind:

- Choose a hosting provider that offers the features and resources that you need.
- Deploy your model to the hosting provider in a way that is secure and scalable.
- Design your API endpoint in a way that is easy to use and efficient.
- Document your API endpoint so that others can easily use it.

Recipe: Increasing the Context Window of an LLM Model

Use cases:

Increasing the context window of an LLM model can improve its performance on a variety of tasks, such as question answering, summarization, and translation.
A larger context window allows the model to better understand the context of the input and to generate more accurate and informative responses.

Function:

There are a few different ways to increase the context window of an LLM model:

Use a larger training dataset: Training an LLM model on a larger dataset can help it to learn a wider range of patterns and to better understand the context of the input.
Use a more powerful training model: Training an LLM model with a more powerful model, such as a GPU cluster, can allow it to process larger datasets and to learn more complex patterns.
Use a technique called context sliding: Context sliding works by breaking the input into smaller chunks and then training the model on each chunk separately. This can allow the model to learn long-range dependencies in the input.

Best ways to implement:

The best way to implement this recipe will depend on the specific LLM model that you are using and the resources that you have available. However, there are some general best practices that you can follow:

If you have access to a large dataset, you can try training the model on the entire dataset. This can be the most effective way to increase the context window of the model.

If you do not have access to a large dataset, you can try using a technique called context sliding. Context sliding can be implemented using a variety of different methods, such as the following:

- Split the input into smaller chunks of a fixed size.
- Train the model on each chunk separately.
- Combine the outputs of the model for each chunk to generate the final output.

Example:
```
# Split the input into smaller chunks of a fixed size
chunks = input.split("\n")

# Train the model on each chunk separately
```

```
outputs = []
for chunk in chunks:
    output = model(chunk)
    outputs.append(output)

# Combine the outputs of the model for each chunk to generate the final output
final_output = "".join(outputs)
```

Tips:

When increasing the context window of an LLM model, it is important to keep the following in mind:

Increasing the context window can improve the model's performance, but it can also make it more computationally expensive to train and deploy the model.
It is important to choose a context window size that is appropriate for the task that you are using the model for. A too small context window may not allow the model to learn the context of the input, while a too large context window may make the model too computationally expensive to train and deploy.
It is important to evaluate the model's performance on a held-out test dataset after increasing the context window to ensure that the improvement in performance is statistically significant.

Recipe: Hyperparameter Tuning for LLM Models

Use cases:

Hyperparameter tuning is the process of adjusting the hyperparameters of a machine learning model to improve its performance.
Hyperparameter tuning is especially important for LLM models, which have a large number of hyperparameters.

Function:

Hyperparameters are parameters that are set before the training process begins. They determine the model's structure and learning speed and need to be tuned to optimally solve the machine learning problem.
Some common hyperparameters for LLM models include:
Learning rate: The learning rate controls how quickly the model learns. A too-high learning rate can cause the model to overshoot the minimum loss, while a too-low learning rate can cause the model to converge slowly or not at all.
Batch size: The batch size controls how many samples are processed by the model at a time. A larger batch size can improve the efficiency of the training process, but it can also lead to overfitting.
Number of epochs: The number of epochs controls how many times the model sees the entire training dataset. A higher number of epochs can lead to better performance, but it can also increase the training time.
Optimizer: The optimizer controls how the model updates its weights during training. There are a variety of different optimizers available, each with its own advantages and disadvantages.

Best ways to implement:

There are a variety of different methods for hyperparameter tuning, but some of the most common methods include:

- Grid search: Grid search involves trying all possible combinations of hyperparameter values from a predefined grid. This can be a computationally expensive method, but it can be effective for finding the best hyperparameter values.
- Random search: Random search involves trying random combinations of hyperparameter values. This can be less computationally expensive than grid search, but it may not be as effective for finding the best hyperparameter values.
- Bayesian optimization: Bayesian optimization is a more sophisticated method of hyperparameter tuning that uses a Bayesian model to learn about the relationship between the hyperparameters and the model's performance. This can be a computationally expensive method, but it can be very effective for finding the best hyperparameter values.

Example:
```python
import random

# Define the hyperparameters that we want to tune
hyperparameters = {
    "learning_rate": [1e-5, 3e-5, 5e-5],
    "batch_size": [16, 32, 64],
    "num_epochs": [5, 10, 15]
}

# Create a random search object
random_search = RandomSearch(hyperparameters)

# Train the model with different hyperparameter values
best_model = None
best_performance = 0
for hyperparameter_values in random_search:
    model = train_model(hyperparameter_values)

    # Evaluate the model on a held-out test dataset
    performance = evaluate_model(model)

    if performance > best_performance:
        best_model = model
        best_performance = performance

# Return the best model
return best_model
```

This example shows how to use random search to tune the hyperparameters of an LLM model. The example defines the hyperparameters that we want to tune and then creates a random search object. The random search object is then used to train the model with different hyperparameter values. The model with the best performance on a held-out test dataset is then returned.

Tips:

When hyperparameter tuning for LLM models, it is important to keep the following in mind:

- LLM models have a large number of hyperparameters, so it can be difficult to tune them all manually. It is important to choose a hyperparameter tuning method that is efficient and that can handle a large number of hyperparameters.

- It is important to evaluate the model's performance on a held-out test dataset after tuning the hyperparameters. This will help to ensure that the model generalizes well to unseen data.
- It is important to be patient. Hyperparameter tuning can be a time-consuming process, but it is important to find the right hyperparameter values to achieve the best possible performance.

Recipe: Hyperparameter Pruning for LLM Models

Use cases:

Hyperparameter pruning is the process of identifying and removing hyperparameters that have little or no impact on the model's performance.
Hyperparameter pruning can reduce the number of hyperparameters that need to be tuned, which can make the hyperparameter tuning process more efficient.
Hyperparameter pruning can also improve the model's performance by removing hyperparameters that are causing overfitting.

Function:

Hyperparameter pruning works by identifying hyperparameters that have little or no impact on the model's performance. This can be done using a variety of different methods, such as:

- Random search: Random search can be used to identify hyperparameters that have a large impact on the model's performance. Hyperparameters that have a small impact on the model's performance can then be pruned.
- Bayesian optimization: Bayesian optimization can be used to learn about the relationship between the hyperparameters and the model's performance. Hyperparameters that have a small impact on the model's performance can then be pruned.
- Gradient-based methods: Gradient-based methods can be used to identify hyperparameters that are causing the model to overfit. Hyperparameters that are causing overfitting can then be pruned.

Best ways to implement:

There are a variety of different ways to implement hyperparameter pruning, but some of the most common methods include:

- Manually pruning hyperparameters: This involves manually identifying and removing hyperparameters that have little or no impact on the model's performance. This can be a time-consuming process, but it can be effective for pruning a small number of hyperparameters.
- Using a hyperparameter pruning library: There are a variety of different hyperparameter pruning libraries available, such as Optuna and Hyperband. These libraries can automate the hyperparameter pruning process and make it easier to prune a large number of hyperparameters.

Example:
```python
import numpy as np
import random
import optuna

# Define the hyperparameters that we want to prune
hyperparameters = {
    "learning_rate": [1e-5, 3e-5, 5e-5],
    "batch_size": [16, 32, 64],
    "num_epochs": [5, 10, 15]
}

# Create a hyperparameter pruning study
study = optuna.create_study()

# Define the objective function
def objective(trial):
    # Get the hyperparameter values from the trial
    learning_rate = trial["learning_rate"]
    batch_size = trial["batch_size"]
    num_epochs = trial["num_epochs"]

    # Train the model with the hyperparameter values from the trial
    model = train_model(learning_rate, batch_size, num_epochs)

    # Evaluate the model on a held-out test dataset
    performance = evaluate_model(model)

    return performance

# Prune the hyperparameters
study.optimize(objective, n_trials=100)

# Get the best hyperparameters
best_hyperparameters = study.best_trial.params

# Train the model with the best hyperparameters
best_model = train_model(*best_hyperparameters)

# Return the best model
return best_model
```

This example shows how to use the Optuna hyperparameter pruning library to prune the hyperparameters of an LLM model. The example creates a hyperparameter pruning study and then defines the objective function. The objective function trains the model with the hyperparameter values from the trial and evaluates the model on a held-out test dataset. The hyperparameters are then pruned using the Optuna optimizer. The best hyperparameters are then used to train the final model.

Tips:

When pruning hyperparameters for LLM models, it is important to keep the following in mind:

- It is important to start with a large number of hyperparameters so that the pruning algorithm has a large pool to choose from.
- It is important to evaluate the model's performance on a held-out test dataset after pruning the hyperparameters. This will help to ensure that the model generalizes well to unseen data.
- It is important to be patient. Hyperparameter pruning can be a time-consuming process, but it can be very effective for improving the model's performance.

Recipe: Transfer Learning for LLM Models

Use cases:

Transfer learning is a machine learning technique where a pre-trained model is used to initialize a new model.
Transfer learning can be used to improve the performance of LLM models on a variety of tasks, such as question answering, summarization, and translation.
Transfer learning can be especially useful for tasks where there is limited data available.

Function:

Transfer learning for LLM models works by initializing the new model with the weights of a pre-trained model. The new model is then trained on the specific task that we want it to perform. The pre-trained model can be a general-purpose LLM model, such as BART or GPT-3, or it can be a task-specific LLM model, such as a QA model or a translation model.

Best ways to implement:

The best way to implement transfer learning for LLM models will depend on the specific model that you are using and the task that you are trying to solve. However, there are some general best practices that you can follow:

- Choose the right pre-trained model: The pre-trained model that you choose should be trained on a large dataset and should be relevant to the task that you are trying to solve.
- Fine-tune the pre-trained model: Once you have initialized the new model with the weights of the pre-trained model, you should fine-tune the new model on the specific task that you want it to perform.
- Evaluate the model on a held-out test dataset: Once you have fine-tuned the model, you should evaluate it on a held-out test dataset to ensure that it generalizes well to unseen data.

Example:
```
import transformers

# Load the pre-trained model
pre_trained_model = AutoModelForQuestionAnswering.from_pretrained("bert-base-uncased")

# Create a new model
new_model = AutoModelForQuestionAnswering.from_config(pre_trained_model.config)

# Initialize the new model with the weights of the pre-trained model
new_model.load_state_dict(pre_trained_model.state_dict())
```

```
# Fine-tune the new model on the QA dataset
new_model.fine_tune("squad")

# Evaluate the model on the QA test dataset
new_model.evaluate("squad")
```

This example shows how to use transfer learning to fine-tune a pre-trained QA model on a QA dataset. The example first loads the pre-trained QA model and then creates a new QA model with the same configuration. The new model is then initialized with the weights of the pre-trained model. Finally, the new model is fine-tuned on the QA dataset and evaluated on the QA test dataset.

Tips:

When using transfer learning for LLM models, it is important to keep the following in mind:

- The pre-trained model that you choose will have a significant impact on the performance of the new model. It is important to choose a pre-trained model that is trained on a large dataset and that is relevant to the task that you are trying to solve.
- It is important to fine-tune the pre-trained model on the specific task that you want it to perform. This will help the model to learn the specific patterns and relationships that are important for the task.
- It is important to evaluate the model on a held-out test dataset to ensure that it generalizes well to unseen data.

Recipe: Grouped Query Attention

Use cases:

Grouped query attention (GQA) is a technique that can be used to improve the performance of LLM models on a variety of tasks, such as question answering, summarization, and translation. GQA works by grouping the input query into multiple groups and then attending to each group separately.
GQA can help the LLM model to better understand the complex relationships between the different parts of the input query.

Function:

GQA works by first grouping the input query into multiple groups. This can be done using a variety of different methods, such as:

- Random grouping: The input query is randomly grouped into a predefined number of groups.
- K-means clustering: The input query is clustered into a predefined number of groups using the K-means clustering algorithm.
- Expert grouping: The input query is grouped by experts who have knowledge of the specific task that the LLM model is being used for.
- Once the input query has been grouped, the LLM model attends to each group separately. This can be done using a variety of different attention mechanisms, such as scaled dot-product attention and additive attention.

Best ways to implement:

The best way to implement GQA will depend on the specific LLM model that you are using and the task that you are trying to solve. However, there are some general best practices that you can follow:

- Choose the right grouping method: The grouping method that you choose will have a significant impact on the performance of the GQA model. It is important to choose a grouping method that is appropriate for the specific task that you are trying to solve.
- Choose the right attention mechanism: The attention mechanism that you choose will also have a significant impact on the performance of the GQA model. It is important to choose an attention mechanism that is appropriate for the specific task that you are trying to solve.
- Evaluate the model on a held-out test dataset: Once you have implemented GQA, it is important to evaluate the model on a held-out test dataset to ensure that it generalizes well to unseen data.

Example:
import transformers
import torch

```
# Load the pre-trained LLM model
model = AutoModelForQuestionAnswering.from_pretrained("bert-base-uncased")

# Implement the GQA attention mechanism
class GQAAttention(torch.nn.Module):
    def __init__(self, config):
        super().__init__()

        # Define the grouping layer
        self.grouping_layer = ...

        # Define the attention layer
        self.attention_layer = ...

    def forward(self, query, hidden_states):
        # Group the query
        groups = self.grouping_layer(query)

        # Attend to each group separately
        attention_output = self.attention_layer(groups, hidden_states)

        # Return the attention output
        return attention_output

# Create a new model with the GQA attention mechanism
new_model = AutoModelForQuestionAnswering.from_config(model.config)

# Add the GQA attention mechanism to the new model
new_model.add_module("gqa_attention", GQAAttention(model.config))

# Fine-tune the new model on the QA dataset
new_model.fine_tune("squad")

# Evaluate the new model on the QA test dataset
new_model.evaluate("squad")
```

This example shows how to implement GQA for a question answering task. The example first
loads the pre-trained LLM model and then creates a new QA model with the same configuration.
The GQA attention mechanism is then added to the new model. Finally, the new model is
fine-tuned on the QA dataset and evaluated on the QA test dataset.

Tips:

When using GQA, it is important to keep the following in mind:

- The grouping method that you choose will have a significant impact on the performance of the GQA model. It is important to choose a grouping method that is appropriate for the specific task that you are trying to solve.
- The attention mechanism that you choose will also have a significant impact on the performance of the GQA model. It is important to choose an attention mechanism that is appropriate for the specific task that you are trying to solve.
- It is important to evaluate the model on a held-out test dataset to ensure that it generalizes well to unseen data.

Recipe: Sliding Window Attention

Use cases:

Sliding window attention (SWA) is a technique that can be used to improve the performance of LLM models on a variety of tasks, such as question answering, summarization, and translation. SWA works by attending to a fixed-size window of the input sequence at a time.
SWA can help the LLM model to better understand the context of the input sequence and to generate more accurate and informative outputs.

Function:

SWA works by first dividing the input sequence into a number of fixed-size windows.
The LLM model then attends to each window separately.
This can be done using a variety of different attention mechanisms, such as scaled dot-product attention and additive attention.
The outputs of the attention mechanisms for each window are then combined to generate the final output of the LLM model.

Best ways to implement:

The best way to implement SWA will depend on the specific LLM model that you are using and the task that you are trying to solve. However, there are some general best practices that you can follow:

- Choose the right window size: The window size that you choose will have a significant impact on the performance of the SWA model. It is important to choose a window size that is appropriate for the specific task that you are trying to solve.
- Choose the right attention mechanism: The attention mechanism that you choose will also have a significant impact on the performance of the SWA model. It is important to choose an attention mechanism that is appropriate for the specific task that you are trying to solve.
- Evaluate the model on a held-out test dataset: Once you have implemented SWA, it is important to evaluate the model on a held-out test dataset to ensure that it generalizes well to unseen data.

Example:
```
import transformers
import torch

# Load the pre-trained LLM model
model = AutoModelForQuestionAnswering.from_pretrained("bert-base-uncased")
```

```python
# Implement the SWA attention mechanism
class SWAAttention(torch.nn.Module):
    def __init__(self, config, window_size):
        super().__init__()

        # Define the attention layer
        self.attention_layer = ...

    def forward(self, query, hidden_states):
        # Split the hidden states into windows
        windows = hidden_states.split(self.window_size, dim=1)

        # Attend to each window separately
        attention_output = []
        for window in windows:
            attention_output.append(self.attention_layer(query, window))

        # Combine the outputs of the attention mechanisms for each window
        attention_output = torch.cat(attention_output, dim=1)

        # Return the attention output
        return attention_output

# Create a new model with the SWA attention mechanism
new_model = AutoModelForQuestionAnswering.from_config(model.config)

# Add the SWA attention mechanism to the new model
new_model.add_module("swa_attention", SWAAttention(model.config, window_size=128))

# Fine-tune the new model on the QA dataset
new_model.fine_tune("squad")

# Evaluate the new model on the QA test dataset
new_model.evaluate("squad")
```

This example shows how to implement SWA for a question answering task. The example first loads the pre-trained LLM model and then creates a new QA model with the same configuration. The SWA attention mechanism is then added to the new model. Finally, the new model is fine-tuned on the QA dataset and evaluated on the QA test dataset.

Tips:

When using SWA, it is important to keep the following in mind:

- The window size that you choose will have a significant impact on the performance of the SWA model. It is important to choose a window size that is appropriate for the specific task that you are trying to solve.
- The attention mechanism that you choose will also have a significant impact on the performance of the SWA model. It is important to choose an attention mechanism that is appropriate for the specific task that you are trying to solve.
- It is important to evaluate the model on a held-out test dataset to ensure that it generalizes well to unseen data.

Recipe: Efficient Fine-Tuning of Quantized Language Models with QA-LoRA

Use cases: This recipe allows for computationally efficient fine-tuning of large pre-trained language models by introducing quantization awareness into the model adaptation process. It enables low-precision integer quantization during fine-tuning while maintaining accuracy.

Function: QA-LoRA integrates quantization with low-rank adaptation of language models. It balances the degrees of freedom between quantization and adaptation by using group-wise operations, allowing integer quantization of weights during fine-tuning.

Best ways to implement:

1. Initialize pre-trained language model: Load the pre-trained weights (e.g. BERT, GPT-2).

2. Set up quantization: Add fake quantization operations and initialize quantization parameters.

3. Introduce adapters: Add low-rank adapter layers to supplement model weights.

4. Group model weights: Reshape weight tensors into groups along output dimension.

5. Share adapters across groups: Share adapter weights across each group of model weights.

6. Quantize weights group-wise: Apply fake quantization to each group of weights separately.

7. Fine-tune model: Train model end-to-end with quantization and adapters.

8. Merge weights: After fine-tuning, merge quantized weights with adapters.

Example:

```
import torch
from transformers import BertModel

# Load pre-trained BERT
model = BertModel.from_pretrained('bert-base-uncased')

# Initialize 8-bit quantization
fake_quant = torch.quantization.FakeQuantize()

# Add LoRA adapter layers
adapter = nn.Linear(512, 512)
```

```
# Group weight tensors into 32 groups
model.weight = model.weight.reshape(-1, 32, 512)

# Share adapters across groups
adapter = nn.parameter(torch.repmat(adapter, 32))

# Quantize each group separately
model.weight = fake_quant(model.weight)

# Fine-tune model end-to-end
# ...

# Merge quantized weights and adapters
model.weight = model.weight + adapter
```

This integrates 8-bit quantization into BERT fine-tuning using shared low-rank adapters applied group-wise. The result is an efficiently fine-tuned model with quantized integer weights.

Chapter 4: Training and Fine Tuning Recipes

Recipe: Training a Large Language Model from Scratch

Use cases: This recipe can be used to train a large language model (LLM) from scratch. LLMs are a type of machine learning model that are trained on a massive dataset of text and code. LLMs can be used for a variety of tasks, such as generating text, translating languages, and answering questions.

Function: This recipe works by feeding a massive dataset of text and code to a neural network architecture. The neural network is trained to predict the next word in a sequence, and over time it learns the patterns in the data. Once the neural network is trained, it can be used to generate text, translate languages, and answer questions.

Best ways to implement:

1. Collect a massive dataset of text and code. This is the most important step, as the quality and quantity of the dataset will have a significant impact on the performance of the LLM. Some sources of large datasets include:
    * The Pile
    * Common Crawl
    * GitHub
    * Wikipedia
2. Preprocess the dataset. This involves cleaning the data, removing outliers, and converting the data to a format that is compatible with the neural network architecture that you will be using.
3. Choose a neural network architecture. There are many different neural network architectures that can be used to train an LLM. Some popular architectures include:
    * Transformer
    * GPT-3
    * Jurassic-1 Jumbo
4. Train the neural network. This involves feeding the dataset to the neural network and allowing it to learn the patterns in the data. This process can take a long time, depending on the size of the dataset and the complexity of the neural network architecture.
5. Evaluate the LLM. Once the neural network is trained, you need to evaluate its performance on a held-out test dataset. This will help you to identify any areas where the LLM needs to be improved.
6. Deploy the LLM. Once you are satisfied with the performance of the LLM, you can deploy it to production. This involves making the LLM available to users so that they can use it to generate text, translate languages, and answer questions.

Example:

To train a GPT-3 model from scratch, you would first need to collect a massive dataset of text and code. You can use the sources mentioned above to collect the dataset. Once you have collected the dataset, you need to preprocess it. This involves cleaning the data, removing outliers, and converting the data to a format that is compatible with the GPT-3 architecture.

Once the dataset is preprocessed, you need to train the GPT-3 model. You can use a variety of different neural network libraries to train the model, such as TensorFlow or PyTorch. The training process can take a long time, depending on the size of the dataset and the complexity of the GPT-3 architecture.

Once the GPT-3 model is trained, you need to evaluate its performance on a held-out test dataset. This will help you to identify any areas where the model needs to be improved. If the model is not performing well, you can try retraining the model with a different dataset or with a different neural network architecture.

Once you are satisfied with the performance of the GPT-3 model, you can deploy it to production. This involves making the model available to users so that they can use it to generate text, translate languages, and answer questions.

Tips:

* Training an LLM from scratch is a challenging task. It requires a lot of resources, such as a large dataset of text and code, a powerful computer, and a good understanding of neural networks and machine learning.
* If you are not able to train an LLM from scratch, you can use a pre-trained LLM. Pre-trained LLMs are LLMs that have already been trained on a massive dataset of text and code. They can be used for a variety of tasks, such as generating text, translating languages, and answering questions.
* There are many different resources available to help you train and deploy an LLM. Here are a few examples:
    * Hugging Face Transformers: A popular library for training and deploying LLMs.
    * Google AI Platform: A cloud-based platform for training and deploying LLMs.
    * NVIDIA Triton Inference Server: A high-performance inference server for LLMs.

Recipe: Fine-Tuning a Pre-Trained Large Language Model

Use cases: This recipe can be used to fine-tune a pre-trained large language model (LLM) for a specific task. LLMs are a type of machine learning model that are trained on a massive dataset of text and code. LLMs can be used for a variety of tasks, such as generating text, translating languages, and answering questions. However, LLMs are not always able to perform specific tasks well without being fine-tuned.

Function: Fine-tuning a pre-trained LLM involves feeding it a dataset of examples of the task that you want it to perform. The LLM is then trained to minimize the loss on the examples. Over time, the LLM learns to perform the task.

Best ways to implement:

1. Choose a pre-trained LLM. There are many different pre-trained LLMs available, such as BERT, GPT-3, and Jurassic-1 Jumbo. Choose an LLM that is appropriate for the task that you want to fine-tune it for.
2. Collect a dataset of examples of the task. This dataset should contain examples of the task that you want the LLM to perform, as well as the corresponding outputs. For example, if you want to fine-tune the LLM for text classification, your dataset should contain text snippets and their corresponding labels.
3. Preprocess the dataset. This involves cleaning the data, removing outliers, and converting the data to a format that is compatible with the LLM that you are using.
4. Choose a loss function. The loss function is a function that measures the error between the predicted output and the actual output. The loss function that you choose will depend on the task that you are fine-tuning the LLM for.
5. Fine-tune the LLM. To fine-tune the LLM, you need to feed it the dataset of examples and allow it to learn to minimize the loss on the examples. This process can take a long time, depending on the size of the dataset and the complexity of the task.
6. Evaluate the LLM. Once the LLM is fine-tuned, you need to evaluate its performance on a held-out test dataset. This will help you to identify any areas where the LLM needs to be improved.
7. Deploy the LLM. Once you are satisfied with the performance of the LLM, you can deploy it to production. This involves making the LLM available to users so that they can use it to perform the task that it was fine-tuned for.

Example:

To fine-tune a BERT model for text classification, you would first need to collect a dataset of text snippets and their corresponding labels. You can use a variety of sources to collect the dataset, such as Wikipedia, Amazon Mechanical Turk, or your own data.

Once you have collected the dataset, you need to preprocess it. This involves cleaning the data, removing outliers, and converting the data to a format that is compatible with the BERT model.

Next, you need to choose a loss function. The loss function that you choose will depend on the task that you are fine-tuning the BERT model for. For text classification, you can use the cross-entropy loss function.

To fine-tune the BERT model, you need to feed it the dataset of examples and allow it to learn to minimize the loss on the examples. This process can take a long time, depending on the size of the dataset and the complexity of the task.

Once the BERT model is fine-tuned, you need to evaluate its performance on a held-out test dataset. This will help you to identify any areas where the model needs to be improved. If the model is not performing well, you can try fine-tuning it for longer or with a different dataset.

Once you are satisfied with the performance of the BERT model, you can deploy it to production. This involves making the model available to users so that they can use it to classify text snippets.

Tips:

* Fine-tuning a pre-trained LLM is a powerful technique that can be used to improve the performance of LLMs on a variety of tasks. However, it is important to note that fine-tuning can also introduce bias into the model. Therefore, it is important to carefully evaluate the performance of the model on a held-out test dataset to ensure that it is not biased.
* There are many different resources available to help you fine-tune a pre-trained LLM. Here are a few examples:
    * Hugging Face Transformers: A popular library for fine-tuning LLMs.
    * Google AI Platform: A cloud-based platform for fine-tuning LLMs.
    * NVIDIA Triton Inference Server: A high-performance inference server for LLMs.

Recipe: Using Adapters to Fine-Tune a Large Language Model

Use cases: This recipe can be used to fine-tune a large language model (LLM) using adapters. Adapters are small neural networks that can be added to an LLM to improve its performance on a specific task. Adapters are particularly useful for fine-tuning LLMs on tasks with limited training data.

Function: Adapters work by supplementing the LLM's weights and improving its performance on a specific task. Adapters are typically trained on a dataset of examples of the task.

Best ways to implement:

1. Choose an adapter architecture. There are many different adapter architectures available. Choose an adapter architecture that is appropriate for the task that you want to fine-tune the LLM for.
2. Add the adapters to the LLM. This process will vary depending on the LLM that you are using. However, most LLMs have a way to add adapters.
3. Collect a dataset of examples of the task. This dataset should contain examples of the task that you want the LLM to perform, as well as the corresponding outputs.
4. Train the adapters. To train the adapters, you need to feed them the dataset of examples and allow them to learn to minimize the loss on the examples. This process can take a long time, depending on the size of the dataset and the complexity of the task.
5. Evaluate the LLM. Once the adapters are trained, you need to evaluate the performance of the LLM on a held-out test dataset. This will help you to identify any areas where the LLM needs to be improved.
6. Deploy the LLM. Once you are satisfied with the performance of the LLM, you can deploy it to production. This involves making the LLM available to users so that they can use it to perform the task that it was fine-tuned for.

Example:

To fine-tune a BART model for question answering using adapters, you would first need to collect a dataset of question-answer pairs. You can use a variety of sources to collect the dataset, such as SQuAD, Natural Questions, and Quora.

Once you have collected the dataset, you need to add adapters to the BART model. There are a few different ways to do this. One way is to use the BART AdapterHub, which is a repository of pre-trained adapters for BART. Another way is to train your own adapters from scratch.

Once you have added the adapters to the BART model, you need to train the adapters on the dataset of question-answer pairs. This process can take a long time, depending on the size of the dataset and the complexity of the task.

Once the adapters are trained, you need to evaluate the performance of the BART model on a held-out test dataset. This will help you to identify any areas where the model needs to be improved. If the model is not performing well, you can try retraining the adapters with a different dataset or with a different adapter architecture.

Once you are satisfied with the performance of the BART model, you can deploy it to production. This involves making the model available to users so that they can use it to answer questions.

Tips:

* Adapters are a powerful technique for fine-tuning LLMs on tasks with limited training data.
* There are many different adapter architectures available. Choose an adapter architecture that is appropriate for the task that you want to fine-tune the LLM for.
* You can use the BART AdapterHub to access pre-trained adapters for BART.
* You can also train your own adapters from scratch.
* It is important to evaluate the performance of the LLM on a held-out test dataset to ensure that it is performing well.

Chapter 5: Department & Function Specific Recipes

Recipe: Predicting Customer Churn

Use cases: This recipe can be used to predict which customers are likely to churn, so that businesses can take steps to retain them.

Function: This recipe works by using machine learning algorithms to analyze customer data and to identify patterns that are associated with customer churn. The machine learning algorithms can then be used to predict which customers are likely to churn in the future.

Best ways to implement: The best way to implement this recipe will depend on the specific machine learning algorithm that you are using and the customer data that you have available. However, there are some general best practices that you can follow:

Choose the right machine learning algorithm: The machine learning algorithm that you choose should be appropriate for the type of customer data that you have available and the type of predictions that you want to make.

Prepare the data: Before you can apply a machine learning algorithm to the data, you need to prepare the data. This may involve cleaning the data, removing outliers, and transforming the data into a format that is compatible with the machine learning algorithm.

Train the machine learning algorithm: Once you have prepared the data, you need to train the machine learning algorithm on the data. This involves feeding the data to the machine learning algorithm and allowing it to learn the patterns that are associated with customer churn.

Evaluate the machine learning algorithm: Once the machine learning algorithm has been trained, you need to evaluate it on a held-out test dataset to ensure that it generalizes well to unseen data.

Use the machine learning algorithm to predict customer churn: Once you have trained and evaluated the machine learning algorithm, you can use it to predict which customers are likely to churn in the future.

Example:
```
import numpy as np
import pandas as pd
from sklearn.linear_model import LogisticRegression

# Load the data
data = pd.read_csv('data.csv')
```

```
# Prepare the data
X = data.drop('churn', axis=1)
y = data['churn']

# Split the data into training and test sets
X_train, X_test, y_train, y_test = train_test_split(X, y, test_size=0.25)

# Create a logistic regression model
model = LogisticRegression()

# Train the model on the training data
model.fit(X_train, y_train)

# Evaluate the model on the test data
accuracy = model.score(X_test, y_test)
print(accuracy)

# Use the model to predict customer churn for the test data
y_pred = model.predict(X_test)

# Calculate the confusion matrix
confusion_matrix = np.zeros((2, 2))
for i in range(len(y_test)):
    if y_test.iloc[i] == 0 and y_pred[i] == 0:
        confusion_matrix[0][0] += 1
    elif y_test.iloc[i] == 0 and y_pred[i] == 1:
        confusion_matrix[0][1] += 1
    elif y_test.iloc[i] == 1 and y_pred[i] == 0:
        confusion_matrix[1][0] += 1
    elif y_test.iloc[i] == 1 and y_pred[i] == 1:
        confusion_matrix[1][1] += 1

# Print the confusion matrix
print(confusion_matrix)
```

This example shows how to use a logistic regression model to predict customer churn. The example first loads the data and then prepares the data by splitting it into training and test sets. A logistic regression model is then created and trained on the training data. The model is then evaluated on the test data and the accuracy is printed. Finally, the model is used to predict customer churn for the test data and the confusion matrix is printed.

Recipe: Optimizing Sales Performance

Use cases: This recipe aims to optimize sales performance by analyzing sales data and identifying key factors that influence successful sales outcomes. It helps businesses make data-driven decisions to improve their sales strategies and boost revenue.

Function: This recipe utilizes data analysis techniques and machine learning algorithms to extract valuable insights from sales data. By identifying patterns and trends in the data, businesses can optimize their sales processes, identify potential leads, and enhance customer relationships.

Best ways to implement: ,

1. Data Collection and Preparation:
   - Gather comprehensive sales data, including customer profiles, purchase history, sales interactions, and lead sources.
   - Cleanse and preprocess the data, handling missing values and outliers, to ensure accurate analysis.
   - Feature engineering: Create relevant features such as customer lifetime value, purchase frequency, and lead response time.

2. Choose the Right Machine Learning Algorithm:*
   - Depending on the nature of your sales data and the problem you want to solve, choose an appropriate algorithm (e.g., regression, decision trees, or neural networks).
   - For lead scoring and customer segmentation, algorithms like clustering and classification (e.g., Random Forest or Gradient Boosting) are effective.

3. Data Analysis and Model Training:
   - Split the data into training and test sets to train and evaluate the model's performance.
   - Analyze the data to identify correlations and patterns that influence sales outcomes.
   - Train the selected machine learning model using the training data to predict sales performance metrics (e.g., conversion rates, sales revenue).

4. Model Evaluation and Optimization:
   - Evaluate the model's performance using appropriate metrics (accuracy, precision, recall, F1-score) on the test data.
   - Optimize the model by tuning hyperparameters and trying different algorithms to achieve the best results.
   - Use techniques like cross-validation to ensure the model's robustness and reliability.

5. Implement Insights to Improve Sales Strategies:
   - Analyze the model predictions and extract actionable insights.
   - Implement data-driven sales strategies based on the model's recommendations.

- Continuously monitor and update the model as new data becomes available to adapt to changing market conditions.

Example:

```
import numpy as np
import pandas as pd
from sklearn.model_selection import train_test_split
from sklearn.ensemble import RandomForestClassifier
from sklearn.metrics import accuracy_score, classification_report

# Load sales data
data = pd.read_csv('sales_data.csv')

# Data preprocessing and feature engineering
# ...

# Prepare features (X) and target variable (y)
X = data.drop('sales_outcome', axis=1)
y = data['sales_outcome']

# Split the data into training and test sets
X_train, X_test, y_train, y_test = train_test_split(X, y, test_size=0.25, random_state=42)

# Create a Random Forest Classifier
model = RandomForestClassifier(n_estimators=100, random_state=42)

# Train the model on the training data
model.fit(X_train, y_train)

# Evaluate the model on the test data
y_pred = model.predict(X_test)
accuracy = accuracy_score(y_test, y_pred)
print(f'Accuracy: {accuracy}')

# Generate classification report for detailed evaluation
print(classification_report(y_test, y_pred))

# Use the trained model for making predictions on new sales data
# ...
```

In this example, a Random Forest Classifier is used to predict sales outcomes based on the prepared sales data. The model is evaluated using accuracy and a detailed classification report to assess its performance. Businesses can use the insights from this analysis to optimize their sales strategies and improve overall sales performance.

Recipe: Customer Segmentation for Targeted Marketing

Use cases: This recipe helps businesses segment their customer base to create targeted marketing strategies. By understanding different customer segments, businesses can tailor their marketing campaigns, product offerings, and communication styles to specific customer needs and preferences.

Function: This recipe utilizes clustering algorithms to group customers with similar traits, behaviors, or purchasing patterns into distinct segments. Businesses can then analyze each segment's characteristics and design personalized marketing initiatives to increase customer engagement and satisfaction.

Best ways to implement:

1. Data Collection and Preparation:
   - Collect diverse customer data, including demographics, purchase history, website interactions, and customer feedback.
   - Clean and preprocess the data, ensuring consistency and resolving any data quality issues.
   - Normalize or scale numerical features to ensure equal weight during clustering.

2. Choose the Right Clustering Algorithm:
   - Select an appropriate clustering algorithm such as K-Means, DBSCAN, or hierarchical clustering based on the dataset's size and complexity.
   - Determine the optimal number of clusters (k) using methods like the elbow method or silhouette score.

3. Feature Selection and Dimensionality Reduction (Optional):
   - If dealing with high-dimensional data, consider dimensionality reduction techniques like PCA (Principal Component Analysis) to reduce the number of features while preserving essential information.

4. Clustering and Customer Segmentation:
   - Apply the chosen clustering algorithm to the preprocessed data to create customer segments.
   - Analyze the clusters' characteristics, such as average purchase value, frequency, and customer preferences, to understand each segment's unique traits.

5. Segment-Specific Marketing Strategies:
   - Develop personalized marketing strategies for each customer segment based on their characteristics.
   - Tailor product recommendations, promotional offers, and communication channels to match each segment's preferences and behaviors.
   - Implement A/B testing to validate the effectiveness of segment-specific campaigns.

6. Monitor and Refine Segments:
   - Continuously monitor customer behavior and feedback to adjust segment definitions and marketing strategies.
   - Use feedback loops and customer surveys to gather insights and refine segment-specific approaches over time.

Example:

```
import pandas as pd
from sklearn.cluster import KMeans
from sklearn.preprocessing import StandardScaler
import matplotlib.pyplot as plt

# Load customer data
data = pd.read_csv('customer_data.csv')

# Data preprocessing: select relevant features and handle missing values if any
# ...

# Standardize features
scaler = StandardScaler()
scaled_data = scaler.fit_transform(data)

# Determine the optimal number of clusters using the elbow method
inertia = []
for i in range(1, 11):
    kmeans = KMeans(n_clusters=i, random_state=42)
    kmeans.fit(scaled_data)
    inertia.append(kmeans.inertia_)

# Plot the elbow curve to find the optimal number of clusters
plt.figure(figsize=(8, 6))
plt.plot(range(1, 11), inertia, marker='o', linestyle='--')
plt.xlabel('Number of Clusters')
plt.ylabel('Within-Cluster Sum of Squares')
plt.title('Elbow Method for Optimal K')
plt.show()

# Based on the elbow curve, choose the optimal number of clusters (k)
k = 4

# Apply K-Means clustering with the optimal k
```

```
kmeans = KMeans(n_clusters=k, random_state=42)
data['cluster'] = kmeans.fit_predict(scaled_data)

# Analyze each cluster's characteristics
cluster_summary = data.groupby('cluster').mean()

# Visualize the clusters (for 2D data, if more dimensions, consider dimensionality reduction)
plt.figure(figsize=(8, 6))
plt.scatter(data['feature1'], data['feature2'], c=data['cluster'], cmap='viridis')
plt.xlabel('Feature 1')
plt.ylabel('Feature 2')
plt.title('Customer Segmentation')
plt.colorbar(label='Cluster')
plt.show()

# Develop and implement segment-specific marketing strategies based on cluster_summary
# ...
```

In this example, K-Means clustering is applied to customer data to create distinct segments. The optimal number of clusters is determined using the elbow method, and the clusters are visualized in a 2D space for illustration purposes. Once the clusters are identified, businesses can design personalized marketing strategies for each segment to enhance customer satisfaction and drive sales.

Recipe: Predictive Sales Forecasting

Use cases: This recipe assists businesses in predicting future sales volumes based on historical data. Predictive sales forecasting enables companies to make informed decisions about inventory management, resource allocation, and sales strategies, ultimately maximizing revenue and minimizing costs.

Function: This recipe utilizes time-series forecasting techniques to analyze historical sales data and predict future sales trends. By understanding past sales patterns, businesses can identify seasonal trends, forecast demand, and optimize their sales and marketing efforts accordingly.

Best ways to implement:

1. Data Collection and Preparation:
   - Gather historical sales data, ideally with timestamps, covering a significant period.
   - Clean the data, handle missing values, and ensure consistency in the timestamps.
   - If there are any outliers, decide whether to remove or transform them based on business context.

2. Exploratory Data Analysis (EDA):
   - Conduct exploratory data analysis to understand the data's distribution and identify any trends, patterns, or seasonality.
   - Visualize the data using line charts, histograms, or seasonal decomposition techniques to identify underlying patterns.

3. Choose a Time-Series Forecasting Model:
   - Select an appropriate forecasting model such as ARIMA (AutoRegressive Integrated Moving Average), SARIMA (Seasonal ARIMA), or Prophet based on the data's characteristics and any identified patterns.
   - Consider using machine learning models like LSTM (Long Short-Term Memory) networks for more complex and non-linear patterns.

4. Train and Validate the Model:
   - Split the data into training and validation sets. Use historical data for training and reserve a portion for validation to assess the model's performance.
   - Train the selected model on the training data and validate it using the validation set.
   - Optimize model hyperparameters, such as lag order in ARIMA or number of epochs in LSTM, for better accuracy.

5. Evaluate and Fine-Tune the Model:
   - Evaluate the model's performance using appropriate metrics such as Mean Absolute Error (MAE), Mean Squared Error (MSE), or Root Mean Squared Error (RMSE).

- Fine-tune the model based on evaluation results. Adjust model parameters or consider additional features if necessary to improve accuracy.

6. Make Predictions and Monitor Performance:
   - Once the model is trained and fine-tuned, use it to make sales predictions for future time periods.
   - Monitor the model's predictions against actual sales data to assess its accuracy and reliability over time.
   - Regularly retrain the model with new historical data to adapt to changing sales patterns.

Example (using ARIMA model):

```
import pandas as pd
from statsmodels.tsa.arima.model import ARIMA
import matplotlib.pyplot as plt

# Load historical sales data with timestamps
data = pd.read_csv('sales_data.csv', parse_dates=['timestamp'], index_col='timestamp')

# Explore the data with visualization and seasonal decomposition
# ...

# Choose appropriate ARIMA parameters (p, d, q)
p, d, q = 3, 1, 2

# Train the ARIMA model
model = ARIMA(data, order=(p, d, q))
model_fit = model.fit()

# Make predictions for the next 'n' periods
n_periods = 12  # Example: predict sales for the next 12 months
forecast = model_fit.get_forecast(steps=n_periods)

# Visualize historical sales and forecasted sales
plt.figure(figsize=(10, 6))
plt.plot(data.index, data['sales'], label='Historical Sales')
plt.plot(forecast.index, forecast.predicted_mean, label='Forecasted Sales', color='red')
plt.xlabel('Date')
plt.ylabel('Sales')
plt.title('Sales Forecasting with ARIMA')
plt.legend()
plt.show()
```

```
# Get forecasted values for further analysis or decision-making
forecast_values = forecast.predicted_mean
print(forecast_values)
```

In this example, the ARIMA model is trained using historical sales data, and predictions are
made for the next 'n' periods (in this case, 12 months). The forecasted sales are visualized
alongside historical sales data to provide a clear understanding of the predicted trends.
Businesses can use these forecasts to plan inventory, allocate resources, and optimize sales
strategies for the upcoming periods.

Recipe: Customer Feedback Analysis for Sales Improvement

Use cases: This recipe focuses on leveraging customer feedback to enhance sales strategies and customer satisfaction. By analyzing customer feedback, businesses can identify areas of improvement, address customer concerns, and optimize their sales processes to provide a better customer experience.

Function: This recipe involves natural language processing (NLP) techniques to analyze textual customer feedback. By extracting valuable insights from customer comments, businesses can identify recurring themes, sentiments, and specific pain points. This analysis enables businesses to make data-driven decisions, improve customer service, and tailor sales approaches based on customer preferences.

Best ways to implement:

1. Data Collection and Preprocessing:
   - Gather customer feedback data from various sources, such as surveys, reviews, social media, and customer support interactions.
   - Clean and preprocess the text data by removing special characters, stopwords, and irrelevant information.
   - Tokenize the text into words or phrases, and consider stemming or lemmatization to standardize words.

2. Sentiment Analysis:
   - Apply sentiment analysis techniques to determine the sentiment (positive, negative, or neutral) of each customer comment.
   - Use pre-trained sentiment analysis models or train your own model on labeled data to classify sentiments accurately.

3. Topic Modeling:
   - Utilize topic modeling algorithms like Latent Dirichlet Allocation (LDA) or Non-Negative Matrix Factorization (NMF) to identify recurring topics or themes in customer feedback.
   - Extract keywords and key phrases associated with each topic to understand customer concerns better.

4. Feedback Categorization:
   - Categorize customer feedback into specific categories, such as product quality, customer service, pricing, or delivery issues.
   - Analyze the frequency and sentiment of feedback in each category to prioritize areas for improvement.

5. Root Cause Analysis and Actionable Insights:

- Identify root causes behind negative feedback by drilling down into specific comments and sentiments.
- Generate actionable insights by understanding the context of negative feedback and brainstorming solutions to address customer concerns.

6. Continuous Feedback Loop:
- Implement a continuous feedback loop where customer feedback is regularly collected, analyzed, and used to make improvements.
- Monitor changes in customer sentiment and feedback trends over time to assess the impact of implemented changes.

Example (using Python and NLTK for sentiment analysis and LDA for topic modeling):

```
import pandas as pd
from nltk.sentiment.vader import SentimentIntensityAnalyzer
from sklearn.feature_extraction.text import CountVectorizer
from sklearn.decomposition import LatentDirichletAllocation

# Load customer feedback data
data = pd.read_csv('customer_feedback.csv')

# Sentiment analysis
sid = SentimentIntensityAnalyzer()
data['sentiment_score'] = data['feedback'].apply(lambda x: sid.polarity_scores(x)['compound'])

# Topic modeling with LDA
vectorizer = CountVectorizer(stop_words='english', max_features=1000)
X = vectorizer.fit_transform(data['feedback'])
lda = LatentDirichletAllocation(n_components=5, random_state=42)
topics = lda.fit_transform(X)

# Assign topics to feedback data
data['topic'] = topics.argmax(axis=1)

# Analyze sentiments and topics for actionable insights
positive_feedback = data[data['sentiment_score'] > 0.2]
negative_feedback = data[data['sentiment_score'] < -0.2]

# Print positive feedback topics and negative feedback topics
print("Positive Feedback Topics:")
for topic_idx in positive_feedback['topic'].unique():
    print(f"Topic {topic_idx}: {', '.join(vectorizer.get_feature_names_out()[i] for i in
lda.components_[topic_idx].argsort()[:-10 - 1:-1])}")
```

```
print("\nNegative Feedback Topics:")
for topic_idx in negative_feedback['topic'].unique():
    print(f"Topic {topic_idx}: {', '.join(vectorizer.get_feature_names_out()[i] for i in
lda.components_[topic_idx].argsort()[:-10 - 1:-1])}")
```
```

In this example, customer feedback data is analyzed using sentiment analysis to determine customer sentiment and LDA for topic modeling to identify recurring themes. Positive and negative feedback topics are extracted, providing businesses with insights into what customers appreciate and where improvements are needed. Businesses can then take targeted actions to address negative feedback and enhance customer satisfaction.
```

Recipe: Customer Service Ticket Categorization

Use cases: This recipe helps customer service departments efficiently manage and categorize customer service tickets. By automatically categorizing tickets, businesses can streamline ticket routing, prioritize urgent issues, and improve response times, leading to enhanced customer satisfaction.

Function: This recipe utilizes natural language processing (NLP) techniques to automatically categorize customer service tickets into predefined categories. By analyzing the text content of tickets, businesses can assign appropriate categories, ensuring tickets are directed to the right department or team for prompt resolution.

Best ways to implement:

1. Data Collection and Preprocessing:
   - Gather historical customer service tickets including the ticket text and associated metadata (e.g., ticket ID, customer name, date created).
   - Clean and preprocess the ticket text by removing special characters, stopwords, and irrelevant information.
   - Tokenize the text into words or phrases, and consider stemming or lemmatization to standardize words.

2. Text Vectorization:
   - Convert the ticket text into numerical vectors using techniques like TF-IDF (Term Frequency-Inverse Document Frequency) or word embeddings (e.g., Word2Vec, GloVe).
   - Vectorization helps represent the text data in a format suitable for machine learning algorithms.

3. Choose a Classifier:
   - Select a suitable classification algorithm such as Naive Bayes, Random Forest, or Support Vector Machine for text classification tasks.
   - Train the classifier using labeled ticket data, where tickets are labeled with their corresponding categories.

4. Training the Classifier:
   - Split the labeled ticket data into training and testing sets.
   - Train the chosen classifier using the training data to learn the relationships between ticket text and categories.
   - Evaluate the classifier's performance on the test data using metrics like accuracy, precision, recall, and F1-score.

5. Fine-Tuning and Validation:
   - Fine-tune the classifier by adjusting hyperparameters for optimal performance.

- Validate the model using a validation dataset to ensure it generalizes well to unseen ticket data.

6. Automated Ticket Categorization:
  - Use the trained classifier to automatically categorize new customer service tickets.
  - Integrate the classification model into the ticketing system to process incoming tickets in real-time.

Example (using Python and scikit-learn for text classification with Naive Bayes):

```python
import pandas as pd
from sklearn.feature_extraction.text import TfidfVectorizer
from sklearn.naive_bayes import MultinomialNB
from sklearn.metrics import accuracy_score, classification_report
from sklearn.model_selection import train_test_split

# Load labeled customer service ticket data
data = pd.read_csv('customer_service_tickets.csv')
X = data['ticket_text']
y = data['category']

# Text vectorization using TF-IDF
vectorizer = TfidfVectorizer(stop_words='english', max_features=1000)
X_vectorized = vectorizer.fit_transform(X)

# Split data into training and testing sets
X_train, X_test, y_train, y_test = train_test_split(X_vectorized, y, test_size=0.2,
random_state=42)

# Train a Naive Bayes classifier
classifier = MultinomialNB()
classifier.fit(X_train, y_train)

# Evaluate the classifier on the test data
y_pred = classifier.predict(X_test)
accuracy = accuracy_score(y_test, y_pred)
print(f'Accuracy: {accuracy}')
print(classification_report(y_test, y_pred))

# Use the classifier to categorize new customer service tickets
new_tickets = ["Issue with product delivery", "Billing discrepancy problem", "Technical support
needed"]
new_tickets_vectorized = vectorizer.transform(new_tickets)
```

```
predicted_categories = classifier.predict(new_tickets_vectorized)
print(f'Predicted categories for new tickets: {predicted_categories}')
```

In this example, customer service ticket data is processed and vectorized using TF-IDF. A Naive Bayes classifier is trained on the labeled data and evaluated for accuracy. The trained classifier can then categorize new customer service tickets into predefined categories based on their text content. This automated categorization process enhances the efficiency of customer service operations by ensuring tickets are directed to the appropriate departments for quick resolution.

Recipe: Customer Sentiment Analysis for Service Quality Improvement

Use cases: This recipe helps customer service departments assess customer sentiment from interactions, such as chat transcripts, emails, or surveys. By understanding customer sentiment, businesses can identify areas of improvement, address customer pain points, and enhance service quality to improve customer satisfaction and loyalty.

Function: This recipe involves sentiment analysis techniques to determine the sentiment (positive, negative, or neutral) of customer interactions. By analyzing the sentiment of customer messages, businesses can gain insights into customer satisfaction levels and identify specific issues or concerns. This information is invaluable for making data-driven decisions to enhance customer service quality.

Best ways to implement:

1. Data Collection and Preprocessing:
   - Collect customer interactions data, including chat transcripts, emails, customer feedback forms, or social media messages.
   - Clean and preprocess the text data by removing special characters, irrelevant information, and anonymizing sensitive data.
   - Tokenize the text into words or phrases and handle negations appropriately for accurate sentiment analysis.

2. Sentiment Analysis:
   - Utilize pre-trained sentiment analysis models or train your own model on labeled data to classify customer messages into positive, negative, or neutral sentiments.
   - Consider using deep learning models (such as LSTM or BERT) for more nuanced sentiment analysis if the data complexity warrants it.

3. Categorize Feedback:
   - Categorize customer messages based on their sentiment and specific issues mentioned (e.g., product quality, customer service response time).
   - Track the frequency of different sentiment categories and issues to identify recurring themes.

4. Root Cause Analysis and Actionable Insights:
   - Analyze negative or neutral sentiment messages to identify the root causes of customer dissatisfaction.
   - Extract keywords or phrases from negative messages to pinpoint common issues or concerns.
   - Generate actionable insights by understanding the context of negative feedback and brainstorming solutions to address customer concerns.

5. Performance Metrics:
   - Monitor key performance metrics related to sentiment analysis, such as the ratio of positive to negative sentiments, customer satisfaction scores, and sentiment trends over time.
   - Regularly review these metrics to gauge the effectiveness of implemented changes and customer service strategies.

Example (using Python and VaderSentiment for sentiment analysis):

```python
from nltk.sentiment.vader import SentimentIntensityAnalyzer

# Sample customer interactions data
customer_interactions = [
    "The customer service was excellent! Very helpful and polite.",
    "I am frustrated with the product quality. It does not meet my expectations.",
    "Thank you for resolving my issue promptly. Great service!",
    "The response time was too slow. I had to wait for hours for assistance.",
    "I appreciate the quick delivery and excellent packaging of the product."
]

# Initialize VaderSentiment analyzer
sid = SentimentIntensityAnalyzer()

# Analyze customer sentiment
sentiments = []
for interaction in customer_interactions:
    sentiment_scores = sid.polarity_scores(interaction)
    if sentiment_scores['compound'] >= 0.05:
        sentiment = 'positive'
    elif sentiment_scores['compound'] <= -0.05:
        sentiment = 'negative'
    else:
        sentiment = 'neutral'
    sentiments.append(sentiment)

# Categorize customer interactions based on sentiment
for i, interaction in enumerate(customer_interactions):
    print(f"Interaction: '{interaction}'")
    print(f"Sentiment: {sentiments[i]}")
    print("---")
```

In this example, customer interactions are analyzed using the VaderSentiment library, which assigns sentiment labels (positive, negative, or neutral) to each interaction. By categorizing customer interactions based on sentiment, businesses can identify positive experiences and areas for improvement, allowing them to take targeted actions to enhance service quality.

Recipe: Customer Service Chatbot Implementation

Use cases: This recipe helps customer service departments implement a chatbot to handle common customer queries and issues. Chatbots can provide instant responses, streamline customer interactions, and free up human agents to focus on more complex tasks. Implementing a chatbot enhances customer service efficiency and responsiveness.

Function: This recipe involves creating a customer service chatbot using natural language processing (NLP) techniques. The chatbot should be able to understand customer queries, provide appropriate responses, and escalate issues to human agents when necessary. It utilizes intents and entities recognition to understand customer intents and extract relevant information for accurate responses.

Best ways to implement:

1. Define Chatbot Use Cases:
   - Identify common customer queries and issues that the chatbot will handle.
   - Determine the scope of the chatbot's capabilities, such as FAQs, order status inquiries, or product information requests.

2. Choose a Chatbot Framework:
   - Select a chatbot development framework or platform like Dialogflow, Microsoft Bot Framework, or Rasa NLU.
   - Consider using pre-trained models and libraries for NLP tasks to simplify the development process.

3. Intent Recognition and Entity Extraction:
   - Define intents (purposes of customer queries) and entities (specific information within queries) relevant to the identified use cases.
   - Use NLP techniques to train the chatbot to recognize intents and extract entities from customer messages.

4. Response Generation:
   - Prepare appropriate responses for each identified intent.
   - Use dynamic responses when necessary, incorporating variables such as order numbers or customer names to personalize responses.

5. Integration with Backend Systems:
   - Integrate the chatbot with backend systems and databases to fetch real-time information if required.
   - Implement APIs or webhooks to connect the chatbot with relevant data sources.

6. User Testing and Training:

- Test the chatbot with sample customer queries to ensure accurate intent recognition and response generation.
- Continuously refine and train the chatbot based on user interactions to improve accuracy over time.

7. Human Agent Escalation:
- Implement a mechanism for escalating customer issues to human customer service agents when the chatbot cannot provide satisfactory responses.
- Ensure a smooth transition between the chatbot and human agents to maintain a seamless customer experience.

Example (using Dialogflow for chatbot development):

1. Define Intents and Entities:
- Define intents such as "OrderStatus", "ProductInquiry", and "FAQ".
- Identify entities like "OrderNumber", "Product", and "Issue".

2. Train the Chatbot:
- Use Dialogflow's training console to provide sample phrases for each intent, including variations customers might use.
- Define entities within the phrases to train the chatbot for entity extraction.

3. Response Generation:
- Configure responses for each intent, incorporating dynamic variables when necessary.
- Use fulfillment options to integrate with backend systems for real-time data retrieval.

4. Testing and Deployment:
- Test the chatbot using the Dialogflow simulator, providing sample user inputs and evaluating chatbot responses.
- Deploy the chatbot to customer service platforms, websites, or messaging apps.

5. Monitoring and Iteration:
- Monitor user interactions and analyze chatbot performance metrics, including accuracy and user satisfaction.
- Analyze user feedback and iteratively refine the chatbot's intents, entities, and responses for continuous improvement.

By implementing a customer service chatbot, businesses can enhance customer interactions, reduce response times, and ensure 24/7 availability for customer queries, ultimately leading to improved customer satisfaction and loyalty.

Recipe: Predicting Employee Turnover

Use cases: This recipe can be used to predict which employees are likely to leave the company, allowing HR departments to take proactive measures for retention and talent management.

Function: This recipe employs machine learning algorithms to analyze employee data and identify patterns associated with employee turnover. By using historical data, the algorithms predict which employees are likely to leave in the future, enabling HR departments to implement targeted retention strategies.

Best ways to implement: The successful implementation of this recipe involves following best practices in machine learning and HR analytics:

1. Collect Relevant Employee Data:
   - Gather historical employee data including demographics, job roles, performance metrics, satisfaction surveys, and any other relevant information.
   - Ensure data privacy and compliance with legal regulations (such as GDPR) during data collection and storage.

2. Define the Target Variable:
   - Define the target variable, often denoted as 'churn' or 'turnover', indicating whether an employee has left the company (1) or stayed (0).

3. Prepare and Clean the Data:
   - Clean the data by handling missing values, outliers, and inconsistencies.
   - Feature engineering: Create relevant features like job satisfaction scores, tenure, number of promotions, and performance ratings.

4. Choose the Right Machine Learning Algorithm:
   - Select appropriate machine learning algorithms for classification tasks. Common choices include logistic regression, random forest, or gradient boosting classifiers.
   - Experiment with different algorithms to determine the one that performs best for your specific dataset.

5. Split Data and Training:
   - Split the data into training and test sets to evaluate the model's performance. Common splits include 70% training and 30% testing data.
   - Balance the dataset if there's a significant class imbalance by using techniques like oversampling or undersampling.

6. Train and Evaluate the Model:
   - Train the selected machine learning model on the training data.

- Evaluate the model on the test data using appropriate metrics such as accuracy, precision, recall, and F1-score.
- Use evaluation metrics to assess the model's performance and adjust hyperparameters as needed.

7. Feature Importance Analysis:
- Conduct feature importance analysis to identify which employee attributes contribute most to turnover predictions.
- Use this information to prioritize areas for HR interventions and employee engagement strategies.

8. Predict Employee Turnover:
- Once the model is trained and evaluated, use it to predict which employees are likely to leave in the future.
- Implement targeted retention strategies, such as personalized career development plans, mentoring programs, or recognition initiatives, for employees identified as high-risk.

Example:

```python
import pandas as pd
from sklearn.model_selection import train_test_split
from sklearn.ensemble import RandomForestClassifier
from sklearn.metrics import accuracy_score, classification_report

# Load employee data
data = pd.read_csv('employee_data.csv')

# Prepare the data
X = data.drop('churn', axis=1)
y = data['churn']

# Split the data into training and test sets
X_train, X_test, y_train, y_test = train_test_split(X, y, test_size=0.3, random_state=42)

# Create a random forest classifier
model = RandomForestClassifier(n_estimators=100, random_state=42)

# Train the model on the training data
model.fit(X_train, y_train)

# Evaluate the model on the test data
y_pred = model.predict(X_test)
accuracy = accuracy_score(y_test, y_pred)
```

```
print(f'Accuracy: {accuracy}')
print(classification_report(y_test, y_pred))

# Feature importance analysis
feature_importances = pd.DataFrame({'feature': X.columns, 'importance':
model.feature_importances_})
feature_importances = feature_importances.sort_values(by='importance', ascending=False)
print(feature_importances)
```

In this example, a random forest classifier is used to predict employee turnover. The model is trained, evaluated, and then used to identify important features contributing to turnover predictions. HR departments can use these insights to implement targeted strategies for employee retention.

Recipe: Predicting Employee Job Satisfaction

Use cases: This recipe can be used to predict the job satisfaction levels of employees, enabling HR departments to identify factors influencing job satisfaction and take measures to improve employee engagement and retention.

Function: This recipe employs machine learning algorithms to analyze employee data and predict job satisfaction levels. By utilizing historical data and various employee attributes, the algorithms predict the satisfaction levels of current employees, allowing HR departments to focus on areas that contribute to higher job satisfaction.

Best ways to implement:

1. Collect Relevant Employee Data:
   - Gather historical employee data including demographics, job roles, compensation, work-life balance indicators, performance metrics, and any other relevant information.
   - Include employee survey responses related to job satisfaction, engagement, and work environment.

2. Define the Target Variable:
   - Define the target variable as 'job_satisfaction_score,' indicating the level of satisfaction on a scale (e.g., 1 to 5), derived from employee survey responses or other satisfaction metrics.

3. Prepare and Clean the Data:
   - Clean the data by handling missing values, outliers, and inconsistencies.
   - Feature engineering: Create relevant features such as years of experience, number of promotions, average working hours, and diversity in team.

4. Choose the Right Machine Learning Algorithm:
   - Select appropriate machine learning algorithms for regression tasks. Common choices include linear regression, decision trees, or ensemble methods like gradient boosting regressors.
   - Experiment with different algorithms to determine the one that performs best for your specific dataset.

5. Split Data and Training:
   - Split the data into training and test sets to evaluate the model's performance. Common splits include 70% training and 30% testing data.
   - Normalize or scale numerical features to ensure fair comparison between them.

6. Train and Evaluate the Model:
   - Train the selected machine learning model on the training data.

- Evaluate the model's performance on the test data using appropriate regression metrics such as mean squared error (MSE) or root mean squared error (RMSE).
- Use evaluation metrics to assess the model's accuracy and adjust hyperparameters as needed.

7. Feature Importance Analysis:
- Conduct feature importance analysis to identify which employee attributes have the most significant impact on job satisfaction scores.
- Use this information to prioritize areas for HR interventions and employee engagement strategies.

8. Predict Job Satisfaction:
- Once the model is trained and evaluated, use it to predict job satisfaction levels for current employees.
- Identify employees with lower predicted satisfaction scores and implement targeted interventions, such as mentorship programs, career development opportunities, or workload adjustments.

Example:

```
import pandas as pd
from sklearn.model_selection import train_test_split
from sklearn.ensemble import GradientBoostingRegressor
from sklearn.metrics import mean_squared_error

# Load employee data
data = pd.read_csv('employee_data.csv')

# Prepare the data
X = data.drop('job_satisfaction_score', axis=1)
y = data['job_satisfaction_score']

# Split the data into training and test sets
X_train, X_test, y_train, y_test = train_test_split(X, y, test_size=0.3, random_state=42)

# Create a gradient boosting regressor
model = GradientBoostingRegressor(n_estimators=100, random_state=42)

# Train the model on the training data
model.fit(X_train, y_train)

# Evaluate the model on the test data
y_pred = model.predict(X_test)
mse = mean_squared_error(y_test, y_pred)
```

```
print(f'Mean Squared Error: {mse}')

# Feature importance analysis
feature_importances = pd.DataFrame({'feature': X.columns, 'importance':
model.feature_importances_})
feature_importances = feature_importances.sort_values(by='importance', ascending=False)
print(feature_importances)
```

In this example, a gradient boosting regressor is used to predict employee job satisfaction
scores. The model is trained, evaluated, and then used to identify important features
contributing to job satisfaction. HR departments can leverage this information to enhance overall
employee satisfaction and engagement levels.

Recipe: Predicting Employee Engagement

Use cases: This recipe predicts the engagement levels of employees, allowing HR departments to identify key factors influencing engagement and implement targeted strategies to enhance workplace satisfaction and productivity.

Function: This recipe utilizes machine learning algorithms to analyze historical employee data and predict engagement levels. By evaluating various employee attributes and survey responses, the model predicts current employee engagement levels, enabling HR departments to focus efforts on areas that positively impact engagement.

Best ways to implement:

1. Collect Relevant Employee Data:
   - Gather comprehensive employee data including demographics, job roles, compensation, performance metrics, feedback from surveys, and any other relevant information related to engagement.

2. Define the Target Variable:
   - Define the target variable as 'employee_engagement_score,' representing the level of engagement on a scale (e.g., 1 to 5) derived from employee surveys or engagement metrics.

3. Prepare and Clean the Data:
   - Cleanse the data by handling missing values, outliers, and inconsistencies.
   - Feature engineering: Create relevant features such as years of service, training hours, frequency of recognition, and team collaboration scores.

4. Choose the Right Machine Learning Algorithm:
   - Select suitable machine learning algorithms for regression tasks, such as linear regression, support vector regression, or neural networks.
   - Experiment with different algorithms to identify the one that best fits the dataset.

5. Split Data and Training:
   - Divide the data into training and test sets for model evaluation. Common splits include 70% training and 30% testing data.
   - Normalize or scale numerical features to ensure fair comparison.

6. Train and Evaluate the Model:
   - Train the chosen machine learning model on the training data.
   - Evaluate the model's performance on the test data using appropriate regression metrics like mean squared error (MSE) or root mean squared error (RMSE).
   - Utilize evaluation metrics to assess the model's accuracy and adjust hyperparameters if necessary.

7. Feature Importance Analysis:
   - Conduct feature importance analysis to identify which employee attributes significantly influence engagement levels.
   - Use this information to prioritize HR interventions, training programs, or recognition initiatives.

8. Predict Employee Engagement:
   - Apply the trained model to predict engagement levels for current employees.
   - Identify employees with lower predicted engagement scores and implement tailored interventions, such as mentorship programs, skill development workshops, or team-building activities.

Example:

```
import pandas as pd
from sklearn.model_selection import train_test_split
from sklearn.ensemble import RandomForestRegressor
from sklearn.metrics import mean_squared_error

# Load employee data
data = pd.read_csv('employee_data.csv')

# Prepare the data
X = data.drop('employee_engagement_score', axis=1)
y = data['employee_engagement_score']

# Split the data into training and test sets
X_train, X_test, y_train, y_test = train_test_split(X, y, test_size=0.3, random_state=42)

# Create a random forest regressor
model = RandomForestRegressor(n_estimators=100, random_state=42)

# Train the model on the training data
model.fit(X_train, y_train)

# Evaluate the model on the test data
y_pred = model.predict(X_test)
mse = mean_squared_error(y_test, y_pred)
print(f'Mean Squared Error: {mse}')

# Feature importance analysis
feature_importances = pd.DataFrame({'feature': X.columns, 'importance':
model.feature_importances_})
```

```
feature_importances = feature_importances.sort_values(by='importance', ascending=False)
print(feature_importances)
```

In this example, a random forest regressor is used to predict employee engagement scores. The model is trained, evaluated, and then used to identify important features contributing to engagement levels. HR departments can utilize this information to enhance overall employee engagement and create a more positive and productive workplace environment.

Recipe: Predicting Inventory Demand

Use cases: This recipe predicts the demand for inventory items, allowing businesses to optimize stock levels, reduce carrying costs, and prevent stock outs or overstocking situations.

Function: This recipe employs machine learning algorithms to analyze historical sales and inventory data to predict future demand for inventory items. By evaluating various factors such as sales history, seasonality, promotions, and external factors, the model forecasts the demand for specific items, enabling businesses to make informed inventory management decisions.

Best ways to implement:

1. Collect Relevant Inventory Data:
  - Gather historical sales data, inventory levels, pricing information, promotions, and external factors like holidays or events that might influence demand.

2. Define the Target Variable:
  - Define the target variable as 'demand,' representing the quantity of items sold within a specific time frame, such as daily, weekly, or monthly.

3. Prepare and Clean the Data:
  - Cleanse the data by handling missing values, outliers, and inconsistencies.
  - Feature engineering: Create relevant features such as historical sales trends, average selling prices, promotional periods, and day-of-week effects.

4. Choose the Right Machine Learning Algorithm:
  - Select appropriate machine learning algorithms for time series forecasting tasks, such as autoregressive integrated moving average (ARIMA), seasonal decomposition of time series (STL), or machine learning models like random forests or gradient boosting.

5. Split Data and Training:
  - Split the data into training and test sets for model evaluation. Time-based splits are crucial for time series forecasting tasks.
  - Normalize or scale numerical features as necessary.

6. Train and Evaluate the Model:
  - Train the selected machine learning model on the training data.
  - Evaluate the model's performance on the test data using appropriate metrics such as mean absolute error (MAE), mean squared error (MSE), or root mean squared error (RMSE).
  - Utilize evaluation metrics to assess the model's accuracy and adjust hyperparameters if necessary.

7. Feature Importance Analysis (if applicable):

- If using machine learning models like random forests or gradient boosting, conduct feature importance analysis to identify which factors significantly influence demand.
- Use this information to optimize pricing, inventory levels, or promotional strategies.

8. Predict Inventory Demand:
- Apply the trained model to predict the demand for specific inventory items.
- Utilize these predictions to optimize inventory levels, plan production schedules, and make informed purchasing decisions.

Example:

```
import pandas as pd
from sklearn.model_selection import train_test_split
from sklearn.ensemble import RandomForestRegressor
from sklearn.metrics import mean_absolute_error

# Load inventory data
data = pd.read_csv('inventory_data.csv')

# Prepare the data
X = data.drop('demand', axis=1)
y = data['demand']

# Split the data into training and test sets (considering time-based split for time series data)
train_size = int(0.8 * len(X))
X_train, X_test, y_train, y_test = X[:train_size], X[train_size:], y[:train_size], y[train_size:]

# Create a random forest regressor
model = RandomForestRegressor(n_estimators=100, random_state=42)

# Train the model on the training data
model.fit(X_train, y_train)

# Evaluate the model on the test data
y_pred = model.predict(X_test)
mae = mean_absolute_error(y_test, y_pred)
print(f'Mean Absolute Error: {mae}')

# Feature importance analysis (for models that support it)
if hasattr(model, 'feature_importances_'):
    feature_importances = pd.DataFrame({'feature': X.columns, 'importance':
model.feature_importances_})
    feature_importances = feature_importances.sort_values(by='importance', ascending=False)
    print(feature_importances)
```

```
```

In this example, a random forest regressor is used to predict inventory demand. The model is trained, evaluated, and then used to identify important features contributing to demand. Businesses can utilize this information to optimize inventory management strategies and ensure adequate stock levels for their products.

Recipe: Calculating ROI on Software Purchases

Use cases: This recipe calculates the Return on Investment (ROI) for software purchases, enabling companies to assess the financial impact of their software investments. By analyzing costs, benefits, and key performance indicators (KPIs), businesses can make data-driven decisions regarding software procurement.

Function: This recipe utilizes financial data and KPIs to calculate ROI for software purchases. By comparing the costs associated with acquiring, implementing, and maintaining the software with the benefits derived from increased efficiency, revenue, or cost savings, the model provides a quantitative measure of the software's financial impact.

Best ways to implement:

1. Collect Relevant Financial and Operational Data:
   - Gather financial data including software acquisition costs, implementation costs, training expenses, and ongoing maintenance fees.
   - Collect operational data such as productivity metrics, time saved, revenue increase, or cost reduction attributed to the software.

2. Define the Target Variable:
   - Define the target variable as 'ROI,' representing the calculated return on investment in percentage or monetary value.

3. Prepare and Clean the Data:
   - Cleanse the financial and operational data by handling missing values, outliers, and inconsistencies.
   - Calculate relevant metrics like net benefit, payback period, or cost savings percentage.

4. Choose the Right Calculation Method:
   - Select appropriate ROI calculation methods based on the nature of benefits. Common methods include net present value (NPV), internal rate of return (IRR), or simple ROI based on the benefit-to-cost ratio.

5. Split Data (if applicable) and Perform Calculations:
   - If historical data is available, split the data into training and test sets for model evaluation.
   - Utilize appropriate ROI calculation methods to compute ROI for each software purchase.

6. Evaluate and Interpret Results:
   - Evaluate the calculated ROI values and interpret the results in the context of the company's financial goals.
   - Assess the impact of software purchases on the company's bottom line and strategic objectives.

7. Compare ROI Across Software Purchases:
   - If analyzing multiple software purchases, compare the calculated ROIs to prioritize investments.
   - Consider other factors such as scalability, vendor reputation, and long-term support in addition to ROI.

8. Make Informed Decisions:
   - Utilize the calculated ROI values and comparison results to make data-driven decisions regarding future software investments.
   - Optimize software portfolios based on financial impact, aligning with the company's overall strategy and budget constraints.

Example:

```
# Sample Calculation of ROI for Software Purchase
acquisition_cost = 50000  # Cost of software acquisition in USD
implementation_cost = 10000  # Cost of implementation in USD
annual_savings = 25000  # Annual cost savings due to software in USD
years = 5  # Number of years for analysis

# Calculate total costs
total_costs = acquisition_cost + implementation_cost

# Calculate total benefits (annual savings over years)
total_benefits = annual_savings * years

# Calculate ROI using the ROI formula: ROI = (Total Benefits - Total Costs) / Total Costs * 100
roi = ((total_benefits - total_costs) / total_costs) * 100

print(f'ROI for the software purchase: {roi}%')
```

In this example, ROI is calculated based on the acquisition cost, implementation cost, annual cost savings, and the number of years of analysis. This simple calculation provides a clear understanding of the financial impact of the software purchase, allowing businesses to assess its viability and make informed decisions.

Recipe: Using Machine Learning to Predict Customer Churn

Use cases: This recipe can be used by finance departments to predict customer churn, which is the rate at which customers stop using a company's products or services. This information can then be used to develop strategies to retain customers and prevent them from churning.

Function: This recipe works by using machine learning algorithms to analyze data about customers and to identify patterns that are associated with churn. The machine learning algorithms can then be used to predict which customers are most likely to churn.

Best ways to implement: The best way to implement this recipe will depend on the specific machine learning algorithm that you are using and the data that you have available. However, there are some general best practices that you can follow:

1. Choose the right machine learning algorithm: The machine learning algorithm that you choose should be appropriate for the type of data that you have available and the type of predictions that you want to make. For example, if you have a lot of historical data about customer behavior, you could use a supervised learning algorithm such as a logistic regression model. If you have less data, you could use an unsupervised learning algorithm such as a clustering algorithm.
2. Prepare the data: Before you can apply a machine learning algorithm to the data, you need to prepare the data. This may involve cleaning the data, removing outliers, and transforming the data into a format that is compatible with the machine learning algorithm.
3. Train the machine learning algorithm: Once you have prepared the data, you need to train the machine learning algorithm on the data. This involves feeding the data to the machine learning algorithm and allowing it to learn the patterns in the data.
4. Evaluate the machine learning algorithm: Once the machine learning algorithm has been trained, you need to evaluate it on a held-out test dataset to ensure that it generalizes well to unseen data.
5. Use the machine learning algorithm to predict customer churn: Once you have trained and evaluated the machine learning algorithm, you can use it to predict customer churn. You can then use this information to develop strategies to retain customers and prevent them from churning.

Example:

Here is a simple example of how to use machine learning to predict customer churn using Python:

```
import pandas as pd
from sklearn.model_selection import train_test_split
from sklearn.linear_model import LogisticRegression
```

```
# Load the customer data
customer_data = pd.read_csv('customer_data.csv')

# Preprocess the data
# ...

# Split the data into training and test sets
X_train, X_test, y_train, y_test = train_test_split(X, y, test_size=0.25)

# Create a logistic regression model
model = LogisticRegression()

# Train the model
model.fit(X_train, y_train)

# Evaluate the model
model.score(X_test, y_test)

# Predict customer churn
churn_probabilities = model.predict_proba(X_test)[:, 1]

# Identify customers who are most likely to churn
churn_threshold = 0.5
churning_customers = X_test[churn_probabilities > churn_threshold]

# Take steps to retain churning customers
# ...
```

This is just a simple example, and there are many other ways to use machine learning to predict customer churn. The best approach for you will depend on your specific needs and the data that you have available.

Tips:

* When using machine learning to predict customer churn, it is important to keep the following in mind:

    * Choose the right machine learning algorithm for your data and your prediction needs.
    * Prepare the data carefully before training the machine learning algorithm.
    * Evaluate the machine learning algorithm on a held-out test dataset to ensure that it generalizes well to unseen data.
    * Monitor the performance of the machine learning algorithm over time and retrain the algorithm if necessary.

Recipe: Using Machine Learning to Detect Fraudulent Transactions

Use cases: This recipe can be used by finance departments to detect fraudulent transactions, such as credit card fraud and insurance fraud. This information can then be used to prevent fraudulent transactions from occurring and to identify and prosecute fraudsters.

Function: This recipe works by using machine learning algorithms to analyze data about transactions and to identify patterns that are associated with fraud. The machine learning algorithms can then be used to detect fraudulent transactions in real time or to identify fraudulent transactions after they have occurred.

Best ways to implement: The best way to implement this recipe will depend on the specific machine learning algorithm that you are using and the data that you have available. However, there are some general best practices that you can follow:

1. Choose the right machine learning algorithm: The machine learning algorithm that you choose should be appropriate for the type of data that you have available and the type of fraud that you are trying to detect. For example, if you have a lot of historical data about fraudulent transactions, you could use a supervised learning algorithm such as a support vector machine (SVM) model. If you have less data, you could use an unsupervised learning algorithm such as an anomaly detection algorithm.
2. Prepare the data: Before you can apply a machine learning algorithm to the data, you need to prepare the data. This may involve cleaning the data, removing outliers, and transforming the data into a format that is compatible with the machine learning algorithm.
3. Train the machine learning algorithm: Once you have prepared the data, you need to train the machine learning algorithm on the data. This involves feeding the data to the machine learning algorithm and allowing it to learn the patterns in the data.
4. Evaluate the machine learning algorithm: Once the machine learning algorithm has been trained, you need to evaluate it on a held-out test dataset to ensure that it generalizes well to unseen data.
5. Use the machine learning algorithm to detect fraudulent transactions: Once you have trained and evaluated the machine learning algorithm, you can use it to detect fraudulent transactions. You can do this by feeding the machine learning algorithm new transaction data and by looking for transactions that are flagged as fraudulent by the algorithm.

Example:

Here is a simple example of how to use machine learning to detect fraudulent transactions using Python:

```
import pandas as pd
from sklearn.model_selection import train_test_split
```

```
from sklearn.svm import SVC

# Load the transaction data
transaction_data = pd.read_csv('transaction_data.csv')

# Preprocess the data
# ...

# Split the data into training and test sets
X_train, X_test, y_train, y_test = train_test_split(X, y, test_size=0.25)

# Create an SVM model
model = SVC()

# Train the model
model.fit(X_train, y_train)

# Evaluate the model
model.score(X_test, y_test)

# Detect fraudulent transactions
fraudulent_transactions = model.predict(X_test)

# Take steps to prevent fraudulent transactions
# ...
```
```

This is just a simple example, and there are many other ways to use machine learning to detect fraudulent transactions. The best approach for you will depend on your specific needs and the data that you have available.

Tips:

* When using machine learning to detect fraudulent transactions, it is important to keep the following in mind:

    * Choose the right machine learning algorithm for your data and your fraud detection needs.
    * Prepare the data carefully before training the machine learning algorithm.
    * Evaluate the machine learning algorithm on a held-out test dataset to ensure that it generalizes well to unseen data.
    * Monitor the performance of the machine learning algorithm over time and retrain the algorithm if necessary.
```

Chapter 6: Automation and Agent Recipes

Recipe: Chained Prompt Processing with Language Models

Use cases: This recipe enables users to chain multiple prompts together within a Language Learning Model (LLM), allowing for a coherent, contextually rich conversation. It's ideal for building interactive chatbots, dialogue systems, or creative writing assistants that engage in multi-turn interactions.

Function: Users input a series of prompts, each representing a part of the conversation or narrative. The prompts are processed sequentially, and the Language Learning Model generates responses considering the context provided by the entire chain of prompts. The final output represents a cohesive, contextually aware response based on the entire conversation.

Best ways to implement:

1. Prompt Chaining Interface:
  - Develop an interface where users can input multiple prompts in sequence. This can be a text box where users enter prompts line by line, specifying the order of the conversation. Alternatively, users can use special markers to indicate prompt breaks within a continuous text input.

2. Context Preservation:
  - Modify the LLM to preserve context across prompts. Ensure that the model understands the sequential nature of the prompts and can maintain context from the previous prompts while generating responses to subsequent ones. This might involve tweaking the model's architecture or using techniques like prompt embeddings.

3. Prompt Delimiter Recognition:
  - Implement a mechanism to recognize and handle prompt delimiters. If users input multiple prompts in a single text block, develop a method to identify and separate the prompts. Regular expressions or specific symbols (e.g., '>>>' to indicate a new prompt) can be used for this purpose.

4. Sequential Prompt Processing:
  - Process prompts sequentially, feeding them one after the other to the LLM. The output of one prompt becomes the context for the next prompt. Ensure that the prompts are processed in the correct order to maintain the flow of the conversation.

5. Context Augmentation (Optional):
  - Optionally, implement context augmentation techniques. For instance, if the conversation involves a character speaking, maintain information about the character's identity, emotions, or

tone across prompts. Augmenting context enhances the depth and richness of the generated responses.

6. Feedback Loop for Context Refinement:
   - Include a feedback loop where users can review the generated response and provide additional context if needed. This iterative process allows users to refine the conversation context, leading to more accurate and contextually relevant responses.

7. Error Handling and Graceful Degradation:
   - Implement error handling mechanisms in case of ambiguous or conflicting prompts. Ensure the system gracefully degrades the conversation quality if it encounters ambiguous input. Clear user prompts or requests for clarification can be part of the error handling strategy.

8. User Guidance for Effective Chaining:
   - Provide users with guidelines on effective prompt chaining. Educate users about how the context is preserved, the importance of clear and concise prompts, and how to structure prompts for coherent conversations.

9. Testing and Iterative Improvement:
   - Test the chained prompt system extensively with diverse conversation scenarios. Gather user feedback and iterate on the system to improve its ability to handle complex, multi-turn interactions. Regular updates based on user interactions enhance the system's performance over time.

10. Integration with External Systems (Optional):
    - Optionally, integrate the chained prompt system with external APIs, databases, or services. This integration can enhance the conversation by allowing the system to pull in real-time data or information based on user prompts, providing dynamic and contextually relevant responses.

Implementing these strategies ensures that the Language Learning Model can process chained prompts effectively, creating interactive and contextually rich conversations that align with user expectations. Regular feedback and iterative refinement are key to enhancing the system's performance and user satisfaction.

Recipe: Connecting an LLM Model to an External System

Use cases: This recipe enables the integration of a Language Learning Model (LLM) with external systems, allowing seamless communication between the LLM and databases, APIs, or other services. This integration can enhance the LLM's capabilities by enabling real-time data retrieval, dynamic content generation, or interactive interactions with external applications.

Function: The LLM interacts with external systems through APIs, database queries, or custom integration layers. It can send requests to external systems, receive responses, and utilize the received data to generate contextually relevant and dynamic responses for users.

Best ways to implement:

1. Identify External System(s):
   - Determine the external system(s) you want to connect the LLM with. This could be a database, a web API, a content management system, or any other service providing relevant data or functionalities.

2. Authentication and Authorization:
   - Set up authentication and authorization mechanisms to ensure secure communication between the LLM and the external system. Use API keys, OAuth tokens, or other secure authentication methods to authenticate requests from the LLM.

3. API Integration (or Database Connection):
   - Implement API integration or set up a database connection based on the external system's specifications. If the external system provides a RESTful API, create functions within the LLM to send HTTP requests (GET, POST, PUT, DELETE) to the API endpoints. If it's a database, configure the LLM to establish a secure connection and execute queries.

4. Data Formatting and Parsing:
   - Format the data sent to the external system and parse the data received from the system. Ensure that the LLM understands the data format expected by the external system and can process the responses accurately. Use JSON, XML, or other standard formats for data exchange.

5. Error Handling and Retry Mechanism:
   - Implement error handling mechanisms to handle situations where the external system is unavailable or returns errors. Set up retry mechanisms with exponential backoff to handle temporary failures. Log errors for debugging and monitoring purposes.

6. Rate Limiting and Throttling:
   - Respect rate limits imposed by the external system to avoid overloading their servers. Implement rate limiting and throttling mechanisms within the LLM to control the frequency of

requests sent to the external system. Consider asynchronous processing for non-real-time tasks to reduce the immediate load on the system.

7. Caching Strategies (Optional):
   - Optionally, implement caching mechanisms to store frequently accessed data retrieved from the external system. Caching can reduce the number of requests made to the external system, improving response times and minimizing latency.

8. Security Measures:
   - Apply encryption and secure communication protocols to protect sensitive data transmitted between the LLM and the external system. Ensure that data privacy and security standards are met, especially when dealing with user-related or confidential information.

9. Testing and Monitoring:
   - Thoroughly test the integration under various scenarios, including edge cases and high loads, to identify and resolve potential issues. Set up monitoring tools to track the integration's performance, response times, and error rates. Regularly monitor the system to ensure it functions correctly and address any anomalies promptly.

10. Documentation and Maintenance:
    - Document the integration process, including API endpoints, data formats, authentication methods, and error handling procedures. Keep the documentation up-to-date. Establish a maintenance plan to address changes in the external system, API updates, or security requirements over time.

Implementing these strategies ensures a robust and reliable connection between the LLM and external systems, allowing the LLM to leverage real-time data, dynamic content, and interactive functionalities, enhancing user experiences and system capabilities. Regular monitoring and documentation are essential for the integration's long-term success and maintainability.

Recipe: Connecting an LLM Model to a SQL Database

Use cases: This recipe facilitates the connection between a Language Learning Model (LLM) and a SQL database, enabling the LLM to retrieve, manipulate, and store data dynamically from a structured database. This integration is valuable for applications where the LLM needs real-time access to data stored in SQL databases.

Function: The LLM interacts with the SQL database using SQL queries. It can retrieve specific data, insert new records, update existing records, or delete records based on user prompts or application requirements. This recipe ensures secure and efficient communication between the LLM and the SQL database.

Best ways to implement:

1. Choose a Suitable Database Library:
   - Select a database library compatible with both your programming language and the SQL database. For example, if you're using Python, libraries like `sqlite3`, `psycopg2` (for PostgreSQL), or `pymysql` (for MySQL) are popular choices.

2. Database Connection Setup:
   - Configure the database connection parameters, including host address, port, database name, username, and password. Use environment variables or configuration files to store sensitive information securely.

   Example (Python with `sqlite3`):
   import sqlite3

   # Connect to the database
   conn = sqlite3.connect('example.db')
   ```

3. Execute SQL Queries:
   - Use the database library to execute SQL queries from the LLM. For read operations, use SELECT queries to retrieve data. For write operations, use INSERT, UPDATE, or DELETE queries to modify the database.

   Example (Python with `sqlite3`):
   # Create a cursor object to execute queries
   cursor = conn.cursor()

   # Execute a SELECT query
   cursor.execute('SELECT * FROM table_name')
   data = cursor.fetchall()
   ```

```
# Execute an INSERT query
cursor.execute('INSERT INTO table_name (column1, column2) VALUES (?, ?)', ('value1',
'value2'))

# Commit changes for write operations
conn.commit()

# Close the connection when done
conn.close()
```

4. Parameterized Queries (Prevent SQL Injection):
   - Use parameterized queries to prevent SQL injection attacks. Parameterized queries ensure that user inputs are treated as data, not executable code.

Example (Python with `sqlite3`):
```
# Using parameterized query to prevent SQL injection
cursor.execute('INSERT INTO table_name (column1, column2) VALUES (?, ?)', (value1,
value2))
```

5. Error Handling:
   - Implement error handling mechanisms to capture database-related errors. Handle exceptions gracefully to prevent application crashes and provide meaningful error messages to users or developers.

Example (Python with `sqlite3`):
```
try:
    # Attempt to execute queries
    cursor.execute('...')
except sqlite3.Error as e:
    # Handle database-related errors
    print("Database error:", e)
```

6. Transaction Management (Optional):
   - For complex operations involving multiple queries, use transactions to ensure data integrity. Transactions allow you to execute a series of queries as a single unit, either committing all changes if successful or rolling back to the initial state if an error occurs.

Example (Python with `sqlite3`):
```
try:
    # Start a transaction
```

```
    conn = sqlite3.connect('example.db')
    cursor = conn.cursor()

    # Execute multiple queries within the transaction
    cursor.execute('...')
    cursor.execute('...')

    # Commit the transaction
    conn.commit()
except sqlite3.Error as e:
    # Rollback the transaction if an error occurs
    print("Transaction error:", e)
    conn.rollback()
finally:
    # Close the connection
    conn.close()
```

Implementing these best practices ensures a secure, efficient, and reliable connection between the LLM and the SQL database. By following these guidelines, you can empower the LLM to dynamically retrieve and manipulate data, enhancing its capabilities and the overall user experience.

Recipe: Connecting an LLM Model to a NoSQL Database

Use cases: This recipe enables the integration of a Language Learning Model (LLM) with a NoSQL database, allowing seamless communication and data exchange. NoSQL databases, such as MongoDB or Cassandra, are suitable for handling unstructured or semi-structured data, making them valuable for applications where the LLM requires flexibility in data storage.

Function: The LLM interacts with the NoSQL database using appropriate NoSQL database libraries. It can perform operations like inserting new documents, querying specific data, updating existing documents, or deleting documents based on user prompts or application requirements. This recipe ensures efficient and dynamic data handling between the LLM and the NoSQL database.

Best ways to implement:

1. Choose a Suitable NoSQL Database Library:
   - Select a NoSQL database library compatible with your programming language and the chosen NoSQL database. For example, if you're using Python and MongoDB, the `pymongo` library is widely used.

2. Database Connection Setup:
   - Configure the database connection parameters, including the host address, port, database name, username, and password. Use environment variables or configuration files to store sensitive information securely.

   Example (Python with `pymongo` for MongoDB):

   from pymongo import MongoClient

   # Connect to MongoDB
   client = MongoClient('mongodb://username:password@host:port/database_name')
   db = client.database_name
   ```

3. Perform Basic CRUD Operations:
   - Use the NoSQL database library to perform Create, Read, Update, and Delete (CRUD) operations. Insert documents, query data, update existing documents, or delete documents based on application requirements.

   Example (Python with `pymongo` for MongoDB):

   # Insert a document
   db.collection_name.insert_one({'key': 'value'})
   ```

```
# Query documents
result = db.collection_name.find({'key': 'value'})

# Update documents
db.collection_name.update_one({'key': 'value'}, {'$set': {'key': 'new_value'}})

# Delete documents
db.collection_name.delete_one({'key': 'value'})
```

4. Error Handling:
   - Implement error handling mechanisms to capture database-related errors. Handle
exceptions gracefully to prevent application crashes and provide meaningful error messages to
users or developers.

   Example (Python with `pymongo` for MongoDB):

```
from pymongo.errors import PyMongoError

try:
    # Attempt database operations
    db.collection_name.insert_one({'key': 'value'})
except PyMongoError as e:
    # Handle database-related errors
    print("Database error:", e)
```

5. Schema Design Consideration (if applicable):
   - NoSQL databases offer schema flexibility, allowing documents with varying structures within
the same collection. Design the document schema based on the application's requirements to
optimize query performance and data retrieval.

6. Indexing (if applicable):
   - If query performance is critical, create appropriate indexes on fields frequently used in
queries. Indexing can significantly improve the speed of data retrieval operations.

   Example (MongoDB Indexing):

```
# Create an index on the 'key' field
db.collection_name.create_index([('key', pymongo.ASCENDING)])
```

7. Transaction Management (if applicable):

- Some NoSQL databases, like MongoDB, support multi-document transactions. If your application requires atomicity for multiple operations, utilize transactions to maintain data consistency.

Example (MongoDB Transactions):

```
with client.start_session() as session:
    with session.start_transaction():
        db.collection_name.insert_one({'key': 'value'})
        db.collection_name.update_one({'key': 'value'}, {'$set': {'key': 'new_value'}})
```

By following these guidelines and best practices, you can establish a robust connection between the LLM and the NoSQL database, allowing seamless data manipulation and retrieval. This integration enhances the LLM's capabilities, making it adaptable to a variety of applications where unstructured or semi-structured data handling is crucial.

Recipe: Deploying an LLM Model to a Kubernetes Cluster

Use cases: This recipe guides you through the process of deploying a Language Learning Model (LLM) to a Kubernetes cluster, enabling scalable, reliable, and efficient inference for natural language processing tasks.

Function: The LLM, typically served as a REST API using frameworks like FastAPI or Flask, is containerized and deployed to a Kubernetes cluster. Kubernetes manages the deployment, scaling, and monitoring of the LLM containers, ensuring high availability and resource optimization.

Prerequisites:
1. A trained LLM model.
2. Dockerized LLM application.
3. Access to a Kubernetes cluster (locally using Minikube or cloud-based like GKE, EKS, or AKS).
4. Kubernetes command-line tool `kubectl` installed and configured.

Best ways to implement:

1. Dockerize the LLM Application:
   - Create a Dockerfile specifying the necessary dependencies, environment setup, and model loading logic.
   - Build the Docker image and push it to a container registry (like Docker Hub or Google Container Registry).

   Example Dockerfile (for a FastAPI application):
   ```Dockerfile
   FROM python:3.8-slim

   WORKDIR /app
   COPY . .

   RUN pip install -r requirements.txt

   CMD ["uvicorn", "main:app", "--host", "0.0.0.0", "--port", "80"]
   ```

2. Create Kubernetes Deployment Configuration:
   - Create a Kubernetes Deployment configuration file specifying the Docker image, ports, replicas, and any environment variables required by the application.

   Example Deployment YAML:

```yaml
apiVersion: apps/v1
kind: Deployment
metadata:
  name: llm-deployment
spec:
  replicas: 3
  selector:
    matchLabels:
      app: llm
  template:
    metadata:
      labels:
        app: llm
    spec:
      containers:
      - name: llm-container
        image: your-registry/llm-image:latest
        ports:
        - containerPort: 80
```

3. Expose the Deployment as a Service:
   - Create a Kubernetes Service to expose the deployed application internally within the cluster.

   Example Service YAML (NodePort for external access):
```yaml
apiVersion: v1
kind: Service
metadata:
  name: llm-service
spec:
  selector:
    app: llm
  ports:
    - protocol: TCP
      port: 80
      targetPort: 80
  type: NodePort
```

4. Apply the Configurations to the Cluster:
   - Use `kubectl apply -f deployment.yaml` and `kubectl apply -f service.yaml` to deploy the application and service to the Kubernetes cluster.

5. Scale and Manage the Deployment:
   - Use `kubectl scale deployment llm-deployment --replicas=5` to scale the LLM application to the desired number of replicas.
   - Monitor the deployment using Kubernetes dashboard or command-line tools to ensure proper functioning and resource utilization.

6. Implement Load Balancing and Ingress (Optional):
   - For production deployments, consider using Load Balancers or Ingress controllers for better traffic management, SSL termination, and domain routing.

7. Update and Rollback:
   - To update the deployed application, build a new Docker image, push it to the registry, and update the Deployment configuration.
   - Use Kubernetes' rollout functionality for seamless updates and rollbacks.

   Example Rolling Update:
   ```bash
   kubectl set image deployment/llm-deployment
llm-container=your-registry/new-llm-image:latest
   ```

8. Implement Health Checks and Monitoring (Optional):
   - Configure liveness and readiness probes to ensure the application's health.
   - Integrate Kubernetes monitoring solutions like Prometheus and Grafana for performance monitoring and alerting.

By following these steps, you can effectively deploy an LLM model to a Kubernetes cluster, ensuring scalability, high availability, and easy management of your natural language processing application.

Recipe: Adding a Security Middle Layer for an LLM Model and Internal Network

Use cases: This recipe provides guidelines for implementing a security middle layer to protect the Language Learning Model (LLM) and the internal network, ensuring secure communication, access control, and threat mitigation.

Function: The security middle layer acts as a shield, controlling traffic between the LLM model and the internal network. It enforces authentication, authorization, encryption, and traffic monitoring, enhancing the overall security posture of the system.

Prerequisites:
1. A deployed LLM model accessible via a network endpoint.
2. Understanding of security protocols like HTTPS, OAuth, and JWT.
3. Knowledge of firewall and access control rules.
4. SSL/TLS certificates for enabling encryption (optional but highly recommended).

Best ways to implement:

1. Implement HTTPS for Secure Communication:
   - Configure the LLM model server to use HTTPS (SSL/TLS) for encrypted communication.
   - Acquire an SSL/TLS certificate from a Certificate Authority (CA) to enable secure, encrypted data transfer between clients and the LLM model.

2. Set Up API Gateway or Reverse Proxy:
   - Deploy an API gateway (like NGINX, HAProxy, or Kong) or a reverse proxy to act as the security middle layer.
   - Configure the API gateway to terminate SSL/TLS, handle client requests, and forward requests to the LLM model server over an internal network.

   Example NGINX Configuration (SSL Termination and Reverse Proxy):
   ```nginx
   server {
     listen 443 ssl;
     server_name llm-api.example.com;

     ssl_certificate /path/to/ssl/certificate.crt;
     ssl_certificate_key /path/to/ssl/private.key;

     location / {
       proxy_pass http://llm-model-server:80;
       proxy_set_header Host $host;
       proxy_set_header X-Real-IP $remote_addr;
   ```

```
            proxy_set_header X-Forwarded-For $proxy_add_x_forwarded_for;
            proxy_set_header X-Forwarded-Proto $scheme;
        }
    }
    ```
```

3. Implement Authentication and Authorization:
   - Enforce authentication mechanisms such as OAuth, JWT (JSON Web Tokens), or API keys.
   - Authorize requests based on user roles and privileges before allowing access to the LLM model.
   - Implement access control lists (ACLs) or RBAC (Role-Based Access Control) to manage authorization rules.

4. Monitor and Log Traffic:
   - Implement logging mechanisms to record incoming requests, responses, and any potential security events.
   - Utilize tools like ELK stack (Elasticsearch, Logstash, Kibana) to centralize and analyze logs for security insights.

5. Implement Rate Limiting and DDoS Protection:
   - Implement rate limiting to prevent abuse of API endpoints. Limit the number of requests per minute from each client to mitigate brute-force attacks.
   - Deploy DDoS protection services or tools to safeguard against distributed denial-of-service attacks.

6. Regularly Update and Patch Security Components:
   - Keep the API gateway, SSL/TLS libraries, and other security components up to date with the latest security patches.
   - Monitor security advisories and apply patches promptly to address vulnerabilities.

7. Conduct Security Audits and Penetration Testing:
   - Regularly conduct security audits and penetration testing to identify and address potential vulnerabilities in the security middle layer.
   - Perform security assessments to ensure compliance with security best practices and industry standards.

8. Implement Intrusion Detection and Response Systems (IDRS) (Optional):
   - Deploy intrusion detection and response systems to monitor network traffic for suspicious activities and automate responses to security incidents.
   - Implement machine learning-based anomaly detection to identify abnormal patterns in network traffic.
```

By following these steps, you can establish a robust security middle layer that safeguards the Language Learning Model and the internal network, ensuring secure and controlled access to the LLM's functionalities while enhancing the overall security posture of your system.

Chapter 7: Performing Alchemy and Mixing Algorithms

These recipes delve into the alchemy of mixing algorithms, demonstrating how various machine learning and optimization techniques can be blended to solve complex problems effectively. Each recipe provides a unique approach, showcasing the versatility and power of combining different algorithms for diverse applications.

Recipe: Ensemble Alchemy

Use cases: This recipe is ideal for scenarios where high predictive accuracy and model robustness are crucial, such as in financial forecasting, customer churn prediction, and recommendation systems.

Function: Ensemble Alchemy focuses on harnessing the strengths of diverse machine learning models by blending their predictions. By combining the outputs of individual models, the ensemble model often outperforms its constituent models, creating a powerful predictive tool.

Best ways to implement:

1. Select Diverse Base Models:
   - Choose base models that are fundamentally different in their approaches. For instance, combine decision trees, neural networks, support vector machines, and linear models. Each model brings a unique perspective to the ensemble.

2. Implement Bagging (Random Forest):
   - Utilize bagging techniques like Random Forest, where multiple decision trees are trained on different subsets of the dataset. Each tree provides a prediction, and the ensemble averages or takes a vote, offering a robust and accurate result.
   - In Python, using the scikit-learn library, you can implement a Random Forest as follows:
   ```python
   from sklearn.ensemble import RandomForestClassifier
   model = RandomForestClassifier(n_estimators=100, random_state=42)
   model.fit(X_train, y_train)
   ```

3. Leverage Boosting (AdaBoost or Gradient Boosting):
   - Apply boosting techniques such as AdaBoost or Gradient Boosting, which focus on correcting errors made by previous models. Weak learners are boosted into strong predictors through iterative training.
   - Example of implementing AdaBoost in Python with scikit-learn:
   ```python
   ```

```python
from sklearn.ensemble import AdaBoostClassifier
model = AdaBoostClassifier(n_estimators=50, random_state=42)
model.fit(X_train, y_train)
```

4. Experiment with Stacking:
   - Experiment with stacking, a technique where predictions from multiple base models become inputs for a meta-model (e.g., linear regression). Stacking often captures intricate patterns that individual models might miss.
   - In scikit-learn, you can implement stacking using the `StackingClassifier` or `StackingRegressor`. Here's a simplified example:
   ```python
   from sklearn.ensemble import StackingClassifier
   from sklearn.linear_model import LogisticRegression
   base_models = [('rf', RandomForestClassifier(n_estimators=100, random_state=42)),
           ('ada', AdaBoostClassifier(n_estimators=50, random_state=42))]
   meta_model = LogisticRegression()
   model = StackingClassifier(estimators=base_models, final_estimator=meta_model)
   model.fit(X_train, y_train)
   ```

5. Fine-Tuning and Cross-Validation:
   - Experiment with hyperparameter tuning and cross-validation to optimize the ensemble's performance. Techniques like grid search or random search can help discover the best set of hyperparameters for each base model.
   - Perform cross-validation to ensure the ensemble's robustness across different subsets of the data.

Outcome:
Ensemble Alchemy produces a meta-model that combines the strengths of various machine learning algorithms. This ensemble model often surpasses the predictive accuracy of individual models. By blending different perspectives and learning strategies, the ensemble becomes a powerful tool for making accurate predictions in diverse and complex real-world scenarios. Remember, the magic lies in the combination of diverse models, each contributing a unique facet to the overall predictive power of the ensemble.

Recipe: Algorithmic Fusion for Anomaly Detection

Use cases: This recipe is invaluable in applications where detecting rare or unusual events is critical, such as fraud detection in financial transactions, network intrusion detection, or quality control in manufacturing.

Function: Algorithmic Fusion for Anomaly Detection leverages the collective intelligence of multiple anomaly detection algorithms to enhance the accuracy of identifying rare patterns or outliers in data. By aggregating results from diverse algorithms, this approach significantly improves the detection capabilities, ensuring a more comprehensive identification of anomalies.

Best ways to implement:

1. Implement Multiple Anomaly Detection Algorithms:
   - Choose a selection of anomaly detection algorithms tailored to your specific use case. This might include Isolation Forest, One-Class SVM, Autoencoders, or any other algorithm suitable for the data and the anomaly patterns you're targeting. Each algorithm should have a unique approach to identifying anomalies, ensuring diversity in the ensemble.

   Example implementation in Python using scikit-learn:
   ```python
   from sklearn.ensemble import IsolationForest
   from sklearn.svm import OneClassSVM
   from sklearn.covariance import EllipticEnvelope

   isolation_forest = IsolationForest(contamination=0.1)
   one_class_svm = OneClassSVM(nu=0.1)
   elliptic_envelope = EllipticEnvelope(contamination=0.1)
   ```

2. Aggregate Anomaly Scores:
   - Combine the anomaly scores generated by individual algorithms for each data point. Common aggregation methods include averaging the scores, weighted averaging based on algorithm performance, or selecting the maximum score as the final anomaly score. Experiment with different aggregation techniques to find the most effective one for your use case.

   Example of score aggregation:
   ```python
   aggregated_score = (isolation_forest_score + one_class_svm_score + elliptic_envelope_score) / 3
   ```

3. Utilize Voting Systems:

- Implement a voting mechanism where each algorithm 'votes' on whether a data point is anomalous. Adjust the voting thresholds based on the confidence levels of individual algorithms. For example, if Isolation Forest and One-Class SVM both flag a data point as anomalous, it's more likely to be an actual anomaly.

Example of implementing a voting system:
```python
if isolation_forest_prediction + one_class_svm_prediction + elliptic_envelope_prediction >= 2:
    predict_anomaly = True
else:
    predict_anomaly = False
```

4. Dynamic Algorithm Selection:
- Use contextual information or meta-features derived from the data to dynamically select the most appropriate algorithm for specific data subsets. For instance, if the data exhibits temporal patterns, certain algorithms might perform better at different times. Regularly assess the algorithms' performance and adjust the ensemble composition based on the changing nature of the data.

Example of dynamic algorithm selection based on data context:
```python
if contextual_info == "Daytime":
    use_algorithm = one_class_svm
else:
    use_algorithm = isolation_forest
```

Outcome:
Algorithmic Fusion for Anomaly Detection creates a robust and adaptive anomaly detection system. By amalgamating the strengths of multiple algorithms and incorporating dynamic algorithm selection, this approach significantly enhances the accuracy of identifying rare events. Whether it's uncovering fraudulent activities, identifying network intrusions, or ensuring product quality, this fusion recipe provides a sophisticated solution to address complex anomaly detection challenges, ensuring businesses stay one step ahead of unusual patterns in their data. Remember, the key lies not only in the diversity of algorithms but also in the dynamic adaptation to the evolving data landscape.

Recipe: Reinforcement Learning Hybridization

Use cases: This recipe is invaluable in applications where intelligent decision-making in complex and dynamic environments is required, such as robotics control, game playing, and autonomous vehicles. By combining the power of reinforcement learning with traditional machine learning models, this approach creates a hybrid system capable of learning from both historical data and real-time interactions with the environment.

Function: Reinforcement Learning Hybridization integrates reinforcement learning algorithms, such as Q-learning, Deep Q Networks, and Proximal Policy Optimization, with traditional machine learning models to harness the unique strengths of both paradigms. Reinforcement learning handles sequential decision-making and explores the environment, while traditional models provide valuable insights through value function approximation or policy improvement guidance. This fusion enhances the agent's learning capabilities and decision-making accuracy.

Best ways to implement:

1. Define State and Action Spaces:
   - Clearly define the environment's state space, representing the observable features or variables in the environment. Likewise, define the action space, which outlines all possible actions the agent can take. Ensure that these spaces are compatible with both reinforcement learning and traditional machine learning models.

2. Hybrid Architectures:
   - Implement hybrid architectures, such as the actor-critic model, which combines both policy (actor) and value function (critic) components. In this setup, the policy network (actor) can be a deep neural network capable of handling complex, high-dimensional inputs, while the value function (critic) can be a traditional regression model like linear regression or decision trees, offering effective value function approximation.

   Example of implementing an actor-critic architecture in Python using TensorFlow and scikit-learn:
   ```python
   # Actor (Policy) Network (Deep Neural Network)
   actor_network = create_actor_network(input_shape, num_actions)

   # Critic (Value Function) Model (Linear Regression)
   critic_model = LinearRegression()
   ```

3. Experience Replay:
   - Implement experience replay buffers, a common technique in reinforcement learning. Experience replay allows the agent to learn from past experiences and interactions with the

environment, enhancing sample efficiency and overall stability of the learning process. Ensure the replay buffer stores both states, actions, rewards, and next states for effective learning.

Example implementation of experience replay buffer in Python:
```python
class ExperienceReplayBuffer:
    def __init__(self, buffer_size):
        self.buffer_size = buffer_size
        self.buffer = deque(maxlen=buffer_size)

    def add_experience(self, experience):
        self.buffer.append(experience)

    def sample_batch(self, batch_size):
        return random.sample(self.buffer, batch_size)
```

4. Reward Shaping:
   - Utilize traditional machine learning models, such as regression or classification models, to provide reward shaping. Reward shaping involves offering intermediate rewards to guide the reinforcement learning agent. These intermediate rewards are based on intermediate states, allowing the agent to receive feedback at multiple points during its decision-making process. This helps the agent learn more quickly and make better decisions in complex environments.

Example of reward shaping using a decision tree regressor in Python:
```python
from sklearn.tree import DecisionTreeRegressor

# Reward Shaping Model (Decision Tree Regressor)
reward_shaping_model = DecisionTreeRegressor()

# Train the reward shaping model on historical data
reward_shaping_model.fit(historical_states, intermediate_rewards)
```

Outcome:
Reinforcement Learning Hybridization creates an intelligent decision-making system that combines the exploration capabilities of reinforcement learning with the guidance and insights provided by traditional machine learning models. By effectively integrating these paradigms, the hybrid agent can learn from past experiences, explore the environment efficiently, and make informed decisions based on both historical data and real-time interactions. This approach significantly enhances the agent's adaptability and decision-making accuracy, making it well-suited for applications requiring intelligent, dynamic responses in complex and evolving environments.

Recipe: Genetic Algorithm Optimization

Use cases: This recipe harnesses the power of genetic algorithms, a type of evolutionary algorithm, to optimize critical aspects of machine learning models, including hyperparameters, feature selection, and even neural network architectures. Genetic algorithms excel in navigating complex solution spaces, making them invaluable tools for finding near-optimal solutions in various optimization problems.

Function: Genetic Algorithm Optimization employs evolutionary principles to efficiently explore the solution space, iteratively refining potential solutions until an optimal or near-optimal configuration is found. By mimicking the process of natural selection, crossover, and mutation, genetic algorithms can significantly enhance the performance of machine learning models.

Best ways to implement:

1. Define the Genetic Algorithm Components:
   - Population Size: Specify the number of potential solutions (individuals) in each generation.
   - Selection Mechanisms: Choose methods for selecting individuals from the population for reproduction. Common selection methods include tournament selection, roulette wheel selection, and rank-based selection.
   - Crossover and Mutation Operators: Design crossover operations that combine genetic material from two parent solutions, creating offspring. Implement mutation operators to introduce small random changes into individual solutions, promoting diversity in the population.
   - Termination Conditions: Define stopping criteria, such as a maximum number of generations or a target fitness score, to halt the optimization process.

2. Encode Solutions:
   - Represent potential solutions (e.g., hyperparameters, feature sets, neural network architectures) as chromosomes, which consist of genes. Develop appropriate encoding and decoding mechanisms to map between the chromosome representation and the actual configurations.

   Example of encoding and decoding hyperparameters for a machine learning model:
   ```python
   # Encoding: Hyperparameters represented as genes in a chromosome
   chromosome = [0.1, 50, 'adam']

   # Decoding: Mapping genes back to hyperparameters
   learning_rate = chromosome[0]
   epochs = int(chromosome[1])
   optimizer = chromosome[2]
   ```

3. Fitness Function:
   - Create a fitness function that evaluates the performance of a solution on the given task. The fitness function quantifies how well a particular configuration solves the problem at hand. This function acts as the guiding force, driving the genetic algorithm toward optimal or near-optimal solutions.

   Example of a fitness function for hyperparameter optimization based on cross-validation accuracy:
```python
def fitness_function(chromosome):
    # Decode the chromosome to obtain hyperparameters
    learning_rate, epochs, optimizer = decode_chromosome(chromosome)

    # Train a machine learning model with the specified hyperparameters
    model = train_model(learning_rate, epochs, optimizer)

    # Evaluate model performance using cross-validation
    accuracy = cross_val_accuracy(model)

    # Return accuracy as the fitness score
    return accuracy
```

4. Evolutionary Process:
   - Implement the key steps of the genetic algorithm: selection, crossover, mutation, and replacement.
      - Selection: Choose individuals from the population for reproduction, favoring those with higher fitness scores.
      - Crossover: Apply crossover operators to selected parent solutions, generating offspring solutions.
      - Mutation: Introduce small random changes into offspring solutions to maintain diversity.
      - Replacement: Replace old individuals in the population with the new offspring, ensuring the population evolves over generations.

   Example of the evolutionary process in a genetic algorithm:
```python
# Initialize population with random solutions
population = initialize_population(population_size)

for generation in range(num_generations):
    # Evaluate fitness of individuals in the population
    fitness_scores = [fitness_function(individual) for individual in population]

    # Select individuals for reproduction using tournament selection
```

```
    parents = tournament_selection(population, fitness_scores)

    # Apply crossover and mutation to create offspring
    offspring = crossover_and_mutation(parents)

    # Replace old individuals with offspring to form the new generation
    population = replace_population(population, offspring)
```

Outcome:
Genetic Algorithm Optimization produces a highly optimized solution for complex machine
learning problems, ensuring that hyperparameters, feature sets, or even neural network
architectures are finely tuned for the specific task. By mimicking the evolutionary process,
genetic algorithms efficiently navigate vast solution spaces, converging toward configurations
that yield optimal or near-optimal performance. This approach significantly enhances the
accuracy, efficiency, and effectiveness of machine learning models, making it an indispensable
tool for data scientists and machine learning practitioners.

Recipe: Hybrid Recommender Alchemy

Use cases: This recipe combines multiple recommendation algorithms, such as collaborative filtering, content-based filtering, and matrix factorization, to create a powerful hybrid recommender system. By leveraging the strengths of each algorithm, this hybrid approach can provide more accurate and diverse recommendations for users.

Function: Implement a hybrid recommendation system that combines collaborative filtering, content-based filtering, and matrix factorization techniques. By blending the outputs of these algorithms, the hybrid recommender system provides personalized and diverse recommendations, overcoming the limitations of individual methods.

Best ways to implement:

1. Implement Collaborative Filtering:
   - Utilize collaborative filtering techniques, such as user-based or item-based collaborative filtering, to capture user-item interactions and identify similar users or items.

2. Incorporate Content-Based Filtering:
   - Implement content-based filtering, where user preferences and item attributes are used to create user and item profiles. Leverage natural language processing (NLP) techniques to analyze textual data associated with items.

3. Apply Matrix Factorization:
   - Utilize matrix factorization methods like Singular Value Decomposition (SVD) or Alternating Least Squares (ALS) to factorize the user-item interaction matrix. Matrix factorization techniques can capture latent features and uncover hidden patterns in the data.

4. Blend Algorithms Using Weighted Averaging:
   - Combine the recommendations generated by collaborative filtering, content-based filtering, and matrix factorization using weighted averaging. Experiment with different weights to find the optimal balance between algorithms. The weights can be determined based on the algorithms' accuracy on validation data or through hyperparameter tuning.

   Example of blending recommendations using weighted averaging:
   ```python
   hybrid_recommendations = (0.4 * collaborative_filtering_recommendations) + (0.3 * content_based_recommendations) + (0.3 * matrix_factorization_recommendations)
   ```

5. Implement Diversity Enhancement Techniques:

- To ensure diverse recommendations, apply techniques such as novelty, serendipity, or diversity-aware matrix factorization. These techniques encourage the recommender system to suggest items that are not only relevant but also diverse and unexpected.

6. Incorporate Feedback Loops:
   - Implement feedback loops where user interactions with recommended items are collected and used to continuously update the hybrid recommender system. Real-time feedback ensures that the system adapts to users' changing preferences and behavior.

Outcome:
The Hybrid Recommender Alchemy recipe results in a recommendation system that outperforms individual algorithms by providing accurate, diverse, and personalized recommendations to users. By combining collaborative filtering, content-based filtering, and matrix factorization techniques, the hybrid approach leverages the strengths of each method, leading to improved user satisfaction, engagement, and retention. This powerful recommender system can find applications in e-commerce, streaming platforms, content delivery services, and more, enhancing user experiences and driving business growth.

Recipe: Sentiment Analysis Alchemy for Social Media Insights

Use cases: This recipe blends natural language processing (NLP) techniques, including rule-based sentiment analysis, machine learning-based sentiment classification, and deep learning-based emotion recognition, to extract nuanced insights from social media data. By combining these algorithms, businesses can understand public sentiment, detect emotions, and identify trends in social media conversations.

Function: Implement a Sentiment Analysis Alchemy system that processes social media text data to categorize sentiments, detect emotions, and uncover underlying themes. By utilizing rule-based approaches, machine learning classifiers, and deep learning models, this system can provide rich and detailed insights into the public's opinions, emotions, and attitudes expressed on social media platforms.

Best ways to implement:

1. Rule-Based Sentiment Analysis:
   - Utilize lexicon-based methods or predefined rules to perform basic sentiment analysis. These rules can involve analyzing words, phrases, or emojis commonly associated with positive, negative, or neutral sentiments.

2. Machine Learning-Based Sentiment Classification:
   - Train supervised machine learning models, such as Support Vector Machines (SVM), Naive Bayes, or deep learning models like LSTM (Long Short-Term Memory) networks, on labeled sentiment data. Use features like word embeddings or TF-IDF vectors to represent text data. Experiment with different algorithms and feature representations to find the most accurate sentiment classifier.

3. Emotion Recognition with Deep Learning:
   - Implement deep learning models, such as Convolutional Neural Networks (CNNs) or Recurrent Neural Networks (RNNs), for emotion recognition. Train these models on emotion-labeled datasets to detect emotions like happiness, anger, sadness, or surprise in social media texts.

4. Blend Rule-Based and Machine Learning Approaches:
   - Combine rule-based sentiment analysis with machine learning classifiers. Use rule-based methods to capture explicit sentiments and machine learning models to handle nuanced or ambiguous expressions. Develop an ensemble system where the final sentiment is determined based on the outputs of both approaches, allowing for a more accurate sentiment categorization.

5. Visualize and Interpret Insights:

- Visualize the results using interactive dashboards or charts to present sentiment distributions, emotional trends, and sentiment changes over time. Incorporate sentiment analysis results into social media monitoring tools to provide real-time insights to businesses and decision-makers.

6. Fine-Tune for Contextual Analysis:
- Fine-tune the models for specific domains or industries. Incorporate domain-specific lexicons or embeddings to improve accuracy, especially when dealing with industry-specific jargon or slang used on social media platforms.

Outcome:
The Sentiment Analysis Alchemy for Social Media Insights recipe results in a comprehensive sentiment analysis system that goes beyond basic positive/negative classifications. By combining rule-based methods, machine learning classifiers, and deep learning models, businesses gain in-depth insights into public sentiments and emotions expressed on social media. These insights can inform marketing strategies, reputation management, customer service improvements, and product development, allowing businesses to stay in tune with public opinions and make data-driven decisions in the dynamic landscape of social media interactions.

www.ingramcontent.com/pod-product-compliance
Lightning Source LLC
LaVergne TN
LVHW051342050326
832903LV00031B/3699